Grave Desire

A Cultural History
of Necrophilia

Grave Desire

A Cultural History
of Necrophilia

Steve Finbow

Winchester, UK
Washington, USA

First published by Zero Books, 2014
Zero Books is an imprint of John Hunt Publishing Ltd., Laurel House, Station Approach,
Alresford, Hants, SO24 9JH, UK
office1@jhpbooks.net
www.johnhuntpublishing.com
www.zero-books.net

For distributor details and how to order please visit the 'Ordering' section on our website.

Text copyright: Steve Finbow 2014

ISBN: 978 1 78279 342 7

A CIP catalogue record for this book is available from the British Library.

Design: Stuart Davies

Printed and bound by CPI Group (UK) Ltd, Croydon, CR0 4YY

We operate a distinctive and ethical publishing philosophy in all
areas of our business, from our global network of authors to
production and worldwide distribution.

CONTENTS

1

Necroduction

Cesare Lombroso—the godfather of criminal anthropology—cites the case of a 40-one-year-old male named Gruyo who lived in Vittoria, Spain. Outwardly, a normal man, married three times, having no previous trouble with the law, Gruyo, over a ten-year period, strangled six women, the majority of them prostitutes. He raped some but mutilated all, severing their intestines and kidneys, pulling the organs out through the vagina.[1] This pre-Ripper perversity, fetishizing the corpse, the body without organs, the organs without body, a sex object devoid of all resemblance to socio-sexual 'norms,' to embedded objects of desire, transmutes the flesh, the bones, the viscera into a sex tool, a mute assemblage of apertures and sites of multiple ingress—a chaos of new vaginas, a variation of mouths, an accretion of anuses. 'In the desiring-machine, one sees the same catatonic inspired by the immobile motor that forces him to put aside his organs, to different parts of the machine, different and co-existing, different in their very coexistence. Hence it is absurd to speak of a death desire that would presumably be in qualitative opposition to the life desires. Death is not desired, there is only death that desires, by virtue of the body without organs or the immobile motor, and there is also life that desires, by virtue of the working organs.'[2]

Born in 1872, Victor Ardisson came from a long line of psychotic criminals. A feeble-minded boy, Ardisson became addicted to masturbation and the consumption of his own semen: 'It would be a pity to lose it,' he said. Local girls spurned his sexual advances. He had a predilection for cunnilingus, liked to suck breasts, and enjoyed licking urine from toilet seats. As he matured, his fetishes grew darker, more extreme. He worked as a stonemason, a gravedigger, and had a spell in the army, deserting on a number of occasions before returning to civilian life. Age was not an obstacle to Addison's desires and compulsions; he disinterred females aged between three and sixty. He sucked the dead bodies' breasts, went down on the corpses; he rarely had vaginal or anal intercourse with the cadavers, nor did he commit acts of mutilation. After a lull in his necrophiliac activities, he watched the funeral of a 17-year-old large-breasted woman in the local cemetery in which he worked. Ardisson exhumed the girl's body, sucked the breasts and performed cunnilingus. His necrophilia out of control, he took for his 'bride' the head of a dead woman. Villagers reported the stench emanating from what turned out to be the decomposing body of a long-dead three-year-old girl; his taste for dead flesh had developed into a sexual desire for the putrescent. After arrest and trial, he enjoyed his time in prison; his favourite meals were cats and rats. Ardisson, a textbook psychopath, felt no remorse, showed no emotional response for his acts.[3] 'Eros and Thanatos are distinguished in that Eros must be repeated, can be lived only through repetition, whereas Thanatos (as transcendental principle) is that which gives repetition to Eros, that which submits Eros to repetition.'[4] Repetition and acceleration, a desire for a corpse as lover, as thing, as tool, an object of love without any chance of reciprocation, without hope of propagation. '[L]ove can be oriented toward its own limit, its own margin: it repeats its own ending. A new love follows, so that each love is serial, so that there is a series of loves. But once again, "beyond" lies the ultimate, at the point where the assemblage changes, where the assemblage of love is superseded by an artistic assemblage.'[5]

In Jörg Buttgereit's 1987 film *Nekromantik*, a woman squats in the grass urinating. The car she is travelling in with her husband crashes and the film's hero—Robert Schmadtke—arrives with his co-workers from Joe's Street-Cleaning Agency to cut the man from the car, bag the woman's viscera, and take the bodies back to the morgue. Robert brings body parts home with him, which he places in pickling jars on a shelf. His girlfriend Betty bathes in blood while Robert watches a television programme on phobias. He fantasizes about the killing of a rabbit, the blow to its head, the knife across its throat, its death kicks. The rabbit is skinned, its eyes excised, its intestines and organ tree removed, then its sexual organs are severed from its body. An unseen man ties the rabbit to a piece of wood, a reverse crucifixion and evisceration. Concurrently, Robert imagines himself operating on a corpse, pulling strips of intestines and other matter from it and placing the offal-like body parts in trays and bloody kidney dishes. These two imagined scenes have Roman Polanski's *Repulsion* (1965) and David Lynch's *Eraserhead* (1977) as their inspiration, a re-imagining of psychological effects and surreal imagery if not pure horror and humour. A man collects apples in an orchard, another man shoots him and then wheels the body away, hiding it in undergrowth. A few months pass, and the cleaning agency are called. Robert steals the body and takes it home where he and his girlfriend Betty caress the putrid corpse, its skin grey and liquefying, its organs protrusive and decaying, its eyes a gelid mess. Betty seems the more excited of the necrophiles, Robert— to begin with—content to watch her, the necrophiliac arousal intensified by scopophilia. The young couple saw off a chair leg, insert it into the decayed genital area of the corpse, roll a condom onto the phallic thrust of wood. Betty undresses and impales herself on the simulated penis. Robert caresses her as she rides and kisses the dead man. As the thanatic threesome move towards climax, in a Bataillean moment, Robert sucks the corpse's eye into his mouth and rolls it around with his tongue, Betty also tastes the eye as it falls from its socket. After Robert loses his job and therefore is no longer able to supply corpses, Betty leaves with the dead body. Angry, Robert sets fire to a photograph of her and kills their cat. Robert pretends he is a corpse, submerged in cold water in the bath, the dead cat's blood turning it red. Death obsesses him—he eats a part of the cat's organs, watches as the moon turns into a skull; he dreams of being dead and playing catch with a head that turns into a piece of meat. In a cemetery, he has unsuccessful sex with a prostitute. He cannot become aroused until he kills her and then fucks her on a gravestone. Discovered by a gravedigger the next morning lying next to the woman's corpse, Robert decapitates the man and watches him die bleeding and twitching. Robert, now in necrophiliac rapture—and in filmic symmetry to the rabbit scene—nails a figure of Christ to a cross; then, in an autoerotic act of necrophilia stabs himself with a large knife, fucking himself with the blade; his cock shooting out jizz as the blade goes in and out. The film of the rabbit, played in rewind, dresses the corpse in its own skin, re-inserts the viscera, bringing the creature alive. He feels inside his own wound and blood spurts from his cock. In the last scene, we see Robert's name on a tombstone and someone wearing woman's slippers digging into the earth with a shovel. *Nekromantik* portrays many levels of necrophilia and the lengths people will go to to fulfil their desires—putrescence, body stealing, rape, voyeurism, and murder among them.

The corpse—or work of art—a polluted object, which, when viewed is sublimated in its observation, where necrophilia incorporates scopophilia, becomes the vision of beauty in excess. Bataille writes about Gilles de Rais: 'His crimes responded to the immense disorder which inflamed him, and in which he was lost. We even know, by means of the criminal's confession, which the scribes of the court copied down whilst listening to him, that it was not pleasure that was essential. Certainly he sat astride the chest of the victim and in that fashion, playing with himself [*se maniant*], he would spill his sperm upon the dying one; but what was important to him was less sexual enjoyment than the vision of death at work. He loved to look: opening a body, cutting a throat, detaching limbs, he loved the sight of blood.'[6]

In his poem 'Paisant Chronicle,' Wallace Stevens writes, 'What it seems / It is and in such seeming all things are.'[7] Meret Oppenheim's *Object* (Paris, 1936) is what it seems—a fur-covered saucer, cup, and teaspoon. What is happening here? The everyday objects we use to consume our oxtail soup and our crème brûlée are fetishized. The fur covering sexualizes the object-in-itself—its new pelt subsumes its very usefulness, its readiness-to-hand. It is transformed from a tool into a sexual object, one of disgust—the thought of fur on our tongues, hairs stuck to the back of our throat, lodged in our oesophagus. Yet, *Object* is also a thing of beauty—the luxurious fur of the Chinese gazelle inviting us to stroke it, the smooth curvilinear architecture of the cup, saucer, and spoon like hypermodern air terminals and airplanes streamlined by hunter-gathering Cro-Magnons; or cars and their eroticized speed deaths, the sexual thrust of the body and its encompassing prosthesis: 'Trying to exhaust himself, Vaughan devised an endless almanac of terrifying wounds and insane collisions: The lungs of elderly men punctured by door-handles; the chests of young women impaled on steering-columns; the cheek of handsome youths torn on the chromium latches of quarter-lights. To Vaughan, these wounds formed the key to a new sexuality, born from a perverse technology. The images of these wounds hung in the gallery of his mind, like exhibits in the museum of a slaughterhouse.'[8] Almost as if Ballard were rewriting the *Second Futurist Manifesto*: 'We declare that the splendour of the world has been enriched by a new beauty—the beauty of speed. A racing car with its bonnet draped with exhaust-pipes like fire-breathing serpents—a roaring racing car, rattling along like a machine gun, is more beautiful than the winged victory of Samothrace'[9] as: 'We declare that the splendour of the world has been enriched by a new beauty—the beauty of death. A racing car with its bonnet draped with genitalia like fire-breathing serpents—an eroticized corpse, rattling along in its death throes, is more beautiful than the crucified body of Jesus Christ.'

Object is an object of desire subject to detestation, of taste subject to distaste, of pleasure subject to pain. Its concave surfaces suggest female sexual organs—it is fiercely anti-masculine, surprisingly political, an inward turning of all those up-thrusting phalluses created by Picasso and Brancusi. 'Very soft particles—but also very hard and obstinate, irreducible, indomitable.'[10] A quotidian object consumed by the sexual gaze of its observer, revulsion overcome by compulsion, rejection by fascination. *Object* destabilizes the phenomenological presentation of everyday objects; defamiliarized in their own appearance of appearance, they question our very being. Meret Oppenheim's *Object* reifies Heidegger's description of phenomena as 'that which shows itself in itself. The manifest.'[11] Is a human body ever reducible to a thing? When does s/he become it? 'The object is an imperative, radiating over us like a black sun, holding us in its orbit, demanding our attention, insisting that we reorganize our lives along its axes. The object is a force, and thus our valuation of it is a gift of force, and nothing like a recognition at all.'[12]

No matter which way you look at them, they look wrong. A head does not seem to fit the body to which it is attached, the legs are not where legs should be, the intagliated pudenda appears alien, distended sockets and dislocated limbs sprout from elongated or truncated torsos. The skin on some of them looks as though it is made from bone, and the bone looks like it's crafted from flesh. 'These flaccid globes, like the obscene sculptures of Bellmer, reminded her of elements of her own body transformed into a series of imaginary sexual organs. She touched the pallid neoprene, marking the vents and folds with a broken nail. In some weird way they would coalesce, giving birth to deformed sections of her lips and armpit, the junction of thigh and perineum.'[13] Some have the faces of young virgins, others resemble department store mannequins, while still more have no heads at all. Most of the bodies are de-articulated, fragmented. Joined at the navel and reversed—the body has two sets of legs, an anus and a hairless vagina where, logically, the head should be. 'In his eye, without thinking, he married her right knee and left breast, ankle and perineum, armpit and buttock.'[14] Another, tied to a banister, is armless, one-legged, the pre-pubescent pudenda juxtaposed against the buttocks as breasts. Where are its arms? What happened to one of its legs? The absence of body parts becomes pure presence through the abject bondage: 'the bodily self is phenomenally represented as inhabiting a volume in space, whereas the seeing self is an extensionless point— namely, the center of projection for our visuospatial perspective, the geometrical origin of our perspectival visual model of reality. Normally this point of origin (behind the eyes, as if a little person were looking out of them as one looks out a window) is within the volume defined by the felt bodily self. Yet, as our experiments demonstrated, seeing and bodily self can be separated, and the fundamental sense of selfhood is found at the location of the visual body representation.'[15] Some might be wearing masks, have leg stumps for a brow, labia for a mouth. Childhood objects surround these figures of erotic amputation, of nightmare assemblage. White ankle socks and patent-leather shoes, blonde locks and pink bows. These mutilated figures are from Hans Bellmer's Doll series originating in 1934 with the publication of *Die Puppe*, ten black and white photographs of the assembled (or disassembled) doll in various provocative poses. 'They must not be opposed determinations of the same of a same entity, nor the differentiations of a single being, such as the masculine and the feminine in the human sex, but different or really-distinct things (*des réellement distincts*), distinct 'beings,' as found in the dispersion of the nonhuman sex, the clover and the bee).'[16]

These examples of perversion—from sexual deviancy, art, film, and literature—these displacements of bodies and body parts, these fetishizations of objects and human beings stem from two main sources –Richard Krafft-Ebing's 1886 psychiatric study of sexual perversions *Psychopathia Sexualis* and Surrealist art from the 1930s. Through an obsession with Surrealist objects: Duchamp's *Why Not Sneeze Rose Sélavy* (1921), Victor Brauner's *The Wolf Table* (1939-47), and Man Ray's *L'Enigme d'Isidore Ducasse* (1920), I discovered Jean Benoît's costumes for *Exécution Du Testament Du Marquis De Sade* (1959). Even more striking than these dark and monstrous assemblages is an object/ costume entitled *The Necrophile [dedicated to Sergeant Bertrand]* (1964-65). My interest in Surrealism brought me to the works of Sigmund Freud and through Freud to Carl Jung, Wilhelm Reich, and the psycho-sexologist Richard Krafft-Ebing. And, here, in the monumental, if now somewhat outdated collection of sexual case histories that make up *Psychopathia Sexualis,* I discovered between the stories of the outwardly normal Gruyo (Case 22) and the psychopath Ardisson (Case 24) the story of the man behind Benoît's necrophile dedication—Sergeant Bertrand. As I read the case history, I wondered what causes a man or woman to want to have sexual congress with a corpse? Is necrophilia the ultimate taboo? Or is it an act of desire perpetrated on an object that is no longer human? To Heideggerize it, where possibility has ended, death resides. With no more actuality, I become a thing—the time of the possibility of impossibility. As in Bataille's fiction and in *Nekromantik,* the I becomes an eye, an object, translated into testes, into an *œuf,* the eye becomes the progenitor of all potential 'I's, of the impossibility of possibility, the conjoined mother/ father of the event of actuality. 'it's an interesting question—in what way is intercourse per vagina more stimulating than with this ashtray, say, or with the angle between two walls? Sex is now a conceptual act, it's probably only in terms of the perversions that we can make contact with each other at all. Sexual perversions are morally neutral, cut off from any suggestion of psychopathology—in fact, most of the ones I've tried are out of date. We need to invent a series of imaginary sexual perversions

8

to keep our feelings alive.'[17]

Haunter of graveyards and morgues, the necrophile embodies our worst fears and our most base desires. In a society in which the image of the corpse is no longer sacred—the huddled bodies of babies twisted like Bellmer dolls on a bloody path in My Lai, the quasi-Ballardian obsession with the remains of Diana, Princess of Wales, Tamil Tiger suicide bombers embracing naked and dead in the back of a truck—the sexual desire for the dead transgresses even the media's exploitation of human mortality. For the necrophile, as embodied in the character of Sergeant Bertrand, the object of desire—what may be my petite brunette or your American sailor—has been supplanted in fantasy and reality by a motionless body, sometimes intact, sometimes bursting at the fleshy seams with gases and insects. 'It's hard to visualize but the day may come when genital sex is a seriously life-threatening health hazard ... At that point the imagination may claim the sexual impulse as its own, an inheritance wholly free of any biological entail. As always with such inheritances there will be any number of new friends eager to help in its spending.'[18] The sublimated purity of so-called normal attraction is superseded, desire is displaced into a simulacrum of the infinite and unknowable other—an ontological seduction, the improbable contradiction of coition between the living and the dead. What drives a man (or woman) to ford a river, climb a wall, risk injury and capture, even his/her own death to dig up a corpse and copulate with it?

From the banks of the Nile, the young slave boy smells the rotting flesh, hears jackals in the hills and fears that the incarnations of Sobek have already found the body. He envisions the crocodiles pulling the woman's body through the papyrus to the river, the twists and rolls, as they tear apart the corpse's arms, legs, head, and torso. Yet, the water remains calm and he walks on through the reeds. The stench increases as he comes to a clearing. He sees the body of Ekibé, wife of SutenAnu, stretched out in the midday sun. One more day, and the embalmers can have her corpse. Her body, once beautiful, is now a bloated writhing mess of flesh. No man would desire congress with it. Surely. He lays down his sling and unwraps his skirt, his penis hard and arched as he moves towards the body.

'Sequence in slow motion: a landscape of highways and embankments, evening light on fading concrete, intercut with images of the young woman's body. She lay on her back, her wounded face stressed like fractured ice. With almost dream-like calm, the camera explored her bruised mouth, the thighs dressed in the dark lace-work of blood. The quickening geometry of the body, its terraces of pain and sexuality, became a source of intense excitement. Watching from the embankment, Travis found himself thinking of the eager deaths of his childhood.'[19]

Throughout history, myth shrouds the necrophile, allied as s/he is with shady religions, shamanism, vampires, and werewolves. Banished to the margins of the real the necrophile is a ghoul, a seer, a shapeshifter, the embodiment of a human monster, devoid of ethics, an anti-moralist—the epitome of evil. This mythologizing, it can be argued, is a means of distancing ourselves from something we do not understand or fear either as an urge within ourselves or as a danger to community and society. As Slavoz Žižek argues in his defence of M. Night Shyamalan's *The Village*, 'We have two universes: the modern, open 'risk society' versus the safety of the old secluded universe of Meaning—but the price of Meaning is a finite, closed space guarded by unnameable monsters. Evil is not simply excluded in this closed utopian space—it is transformed into a mythic threat with which the community establishes a temporary truce and against which it has to maintain a permanent state of emergency.'[20]

The necrophile becomes a mythical monster in order for society to maintain a moral status quo. Necrophilia becomes the ultimate fetish, the last paraphilia, and the weather gauge for society's moral storms.

Fifteen hundred years ago, in a valley close to the north-eastern coast of Peru, near to where in 1534 the Conquistadors would build the city of Trujillo, a Mocha artisan puts aside the vases depicting scenes of anal and oral sex he has made for the priests and the lords. He takes up a thin blade and uses it to roughly incise the leathery clay of the unfired pot. Later, having watched the costumed lords and priests drink the blood of the captive warriors, he pulls the pot from a smoking pit, on the surface, earth-red on cream, is a fine-line drawing of a voluptuous woman her hands encircling an erect penis — the woman is masturbating a skeleton.

'Sex, of course, remains our continuing preoccupation. As you and I know, the act of intercourse is now always a model for something else. What will follow is the psychopathology of sex, relationships so lunar and abstract that people become mere extensions of the geometries of situations. This will allow the exploration, without any taint of guilt, of every aspect of sexual psychopathology. Travis, for example, has posted a series of new sexual deviations, of a wholly conceptual character, in an attempt to surmount this death of affect.'[21]

Facts about Sergeant Bertrand's life are sketchy but using medical and historical records, literature, art, and other case studies, this book hopes to flesh out an analysis of his mania. The details lead to a study of Bertrand and historical necrophiles: from Ancient Egypt, the Moche Civilization of northern Peru, and Herodotus to modern necrophiles such as Carl Tanzler, Gary Ridgway, Mark Dixie, Ted Bundy, and Dennis Nilsen. Charles Dickens, Guy de Maupassant, Joris-Karl Huysmans, Angela Carter, Colin Wilson, Cormac McCarthy, and J.G. Ballard have all written about necrophiles and/or necrophilia, and the necrophile plays a significant role in the Gothic tradition and in Surrealism. The ultimate transgressive act has interested writers from Homer, through the Marquis De Sade, Edgar Allan Poe, Oscar

Wilde, and Charles Swinburne to contemporary novelists such as Poppy Z. Brite, Chuck Palahniuk, and Joyce Carol Oates. The image of the necrophile has inspired Aubrey Beardsley, Gustave Moreau, Salvador Dali, and Jean Benoît. Films as diverse as *Re-Animator*, *Corpse Bride*, *Clerks*, *Weekend at Bernie's* and Katashi Miike's *Visitor Q* have used necrophilia for dramatic or comedic purposes. Popular television series such as *True Blood*, *Family Guy* and *Two and a Half Men* have touched on the subject, while in *CSI: NY*'s second season, a plotline in the episode 'Necrophilia Americana', involved a woman's body found surrounded by American carrion beetles (Necrophila americana), the only witness being a young boy who may or may not have interfered with the body. Japanese anime and manga feature many necrophiles or characters with necrophiliac tendencies. Using these as embedded interpretations in the text, the 'art' of necrophilia—in a necrophagic way, eating its body from the tail (tale) onward—provides a cultural response to the medico-legal aspects and psychological analysis of the men and women drawn to sex with dead bodies.

Dear Reader, I have now laid out her body on her bed—my soror mystica—Rebecca Vaughan, my life, my wife in her death. Here among the mercury fumes, the aqua regia, the potash and the lime, here where I dabble with ampulla and horn of Hermes, with dung bath and crucible, I think of her. No Satanic rites to raise the dead, no kabbalistic moulding of material from the spirit, but a Rosicrucian rebirth, the transmigration of her soul through sexual intercourse. I take my lamp and walk up the narrow steps to her chamber. I feel the vibration of her spirit, the coolness of her matter. I lift the veil, kiss her lips, and enter her house of light. '…it seems likely that our familiar perversions will soon come to an end, if only because their equivalents are too readily available in strange stair angles, in the mysterious eroticism of overpasses, in distortions of gesture and posture. As the logical fashion, such once popular perversions as paedophilia and sodomy will become derided clichés, as amusing as pottery ducks on suburban walls.'[22]

How have our philosophers, psychoanalysts, and cultural thinkers dealt with the question of necrophilia? Bertrand's actions, and necrophilia in general, can be approached using the theories of psychoanalysts and philosophers such as Richard Krafft-Ebing, Sigmund Freud, Georges Bataille, Martin Heidegger, Jacques Lacan, Michel Foucault, Gilles Deleuze, Félix Guattari, and Slavoz Žižek. Throughout the book, I will use quotes—sometimes analytical, sometimes illustrative—from philosophy, psychoanalysis, and literature in an attempt to provide an analysis of necrophilia as revolt, as sickness, or as an extreme normality. 'Violence is the conceptualization of pain. By the same token, psychopathology is the conceptual system of sex.'[23] Reality or myth, perversion or human practice grounded in history and being—these are notes toward an ethics of necrophilia drawn from the dark desires of a nineteenth-century soldier whose acts of violence, corporal defilations, transcendent acts of disgust, bring into question the limits of desire, illuminating, as they do, the erotics of desecration, and a revolutionary view of human rationality. '[V]iolence, and all violence for that matter, reflects the neutral exploration of sensation that is taking place now, within sex as elsewhere, and the sense that the perversions are valuable precisely because they provide a readily accessible anthology of exploratory techniques.'[24]

As a twentieth-century necrophile, Mark Dixie may have put it in his quotidian terms, 'I'd had some toot and a few pints, me and a few friends were celebrating in the Balmoral Castle. It was my 35th birthday. I was staying overnight at someone's flat but went out at three in the morning to see what I could find. I saw a woman by the recreation grounds. I tried to pull her out of her car but some interfering van driver got involved so I shot off. All I got was her useless mobile. I saw another girl—long blonde hair, petite—arguing with her boyfriend. I waited and when she was alone, I stabbed her six or seven times. Bit her an' all. She died right there in the drive. I unzipped and lifted her dress.'

How are these acts possible? Will a sexuality that stands opposed to the possibilities of society, in opposition to procreation, that sickens our minds, that has the potential to destroy life in its desire for death, be forever marginalized because of its degeneration? Should we consider this extreme act of individuation (although endemic in past cultures) a perversion or a representation of human divergence? After all, 'This fundamental differenciation (quality-extensity) can find its reason only in the great synthesis of Memory which allows all the degrees of difference to coexist as degrees of relaxation and contraction, and rediscovers at the heart of duration the implicated order of that intensity which had been denounced provisionally and from without.'[25] Is there some place in our memory where necrophilia is a rite of passage? Somewhere to enact the 'fundamental differenciation' between life and death? An arena in which life 'the heart of duration' seeds death to help it on its way? Or is this sexual intensity, this coexistence of potential life with death, always to be denounced as dark and desperate? After all, as Ballard states, '...the sexual imagination is unlimited in scope and metaphoric power, and can never be successfully repressed.'[26]

2

Necrophilia—Deathinition

Necrophilia (love of the dead)—also called Thanatophilia—is one of the last great taboos of humankind. A paraphilia combining both Eros and Thanatos, necrophilia is a nihilistic act of procreation and an elevation of the corpse to a level of desire, it is an overstepping of traditional ethics and a re-evaluation of sexuality, it is foremost an intricate constituent of human history, religion, and culture: '[J]ust as I finished, I began to feel that icy screaming in one of my auricles, and my blood pumping it all over me until I understood the putrid green stench of that mindless decay…'[27]

So, what is necrophilia? The *Compact Oxford English Dictionary* defines it as: 'necrophilia /nekrəfilliə/ • noun—sexual intercourse with or attraction towards a corpse.' This compact description provides a basis for an examination of the term and its linguistic and legal definition. νεκρός (nekros) = 'corpse' or 'dead' and φιλία (philia) = 'love' or 'friendship', hence an artificial compound word derived from Ancient Greek meaning a love of the dead. The pioneer Belgian psychiatrist Dr Joseph Guislain neologized the word in 1860, but its meaning is closer to a 'love of death' or a 'lust to create death' rather than 'a lover of the dead'. In 1874, W.A.F. Browne, once Commissioner for Lunacy in Scotland, used the term 'necrophagy' (eating of dead or decaying flesh). Alexis Epaulard in his paper 'Vampirisme, Necrophilie, Necrosadisme, Necrophagie' (1901), defined Necrosadism (sexual gratification from the mutilation of corpses). These terminologies often overlap and, in Bertrand's case, they form part of a sexual trilogy in which necrophagy and necrosadism combine to create necrophilia: 'When you put it that way, you would think that people would naturally prefer to be a sex object. After all, to say that your body becomes a waste object is to say that when you die you become excrement. The cadaver is a parody of you made out of shit. Who wants that? Wouldn't it be better to be a sex object?[28] Merriam-Webster's online dictionary defines necrophilia as an 'obsession with and usually erotic interest in or stimulation by corpses'. This takes necrophilia out of the list of paraphilias and places it in the realm of obsession (a weaker form of fetishism). Being obsessed with corpses does not necessarily mean having sex with the dead. Goths wear skull rings and skeleton jewellery. Mexicans celebrate *El Día de los Muertos* (Day of the Dead) where one can buy candy skulls and skeleton dolls.

'I pull back the curtains to reveal a wonderful new world—a party, a riot, a ball. It's the costume affair, Mardi Gras, the Halloween festival, the Day of the dead, and it's enormous fun to prance around on the arm of inevitable doom. Life is short! Seize the day! Go ahead, darling. Slip me on. Pretend you're me. See the world through my sockets. Laugh. Live. Love—while you can. Eat, drink, and be merry. What do you think I do? I'm death, and I laugh and make merry too. I dance with skeletons to make goblets out of skulls—to drink from the cranium, you should know, is very fine.'[29]

Medical definitions: Dorland's Medical Dictionary for Health Consumers (2007) defines necrophilia as 'sexual attraction to or sexual contact with dead bodies.' *The American Heritage Medical Dictionary* (2007) as 'An abnormal fondness for being in the presence of dead bodies and sexual contact with or erotic desire for dead bodies.' Whereas *Mosby's Medical Dictionary, 8ᵗʰ edition* (2009) describes it as 'a morbid liking for being with dead bodies and a morbid desire to have sexual contact with a dead body, usually of men to perform a sexual act with a dead woman.' *The McGraw-Hill Concise Dictionary of Modern Medicine* (2002) puts it more succinctly: 'A paraphilia in which sexuoerotism requires a corpse, which may involve engaging in sexual activity with same' or 'getting a stiffie with a stiff.'

> Did that vengeful man whom, living, you could not gratify,
> In spite of so much love
> Heap upon your indolent, accommodating flesh
> The size of his desire?

> Answer, O violated corpse! and raising yourself with feverish
> arm
> By your stiff braids,
> Tell me, terrifying head, did he press upon your cold teeth
> His final farewells?[30]

The American Psychiatric Association's Diagnostic and Statistical Manual of Mental Disorders classifies necrophilia as a paraphilia or 'recurrent, intense sexual urges, fantasies, or behaviours that involve unusual objects, activities, or situations and cause clinically significant distress or impairment in social, occupational, or other important areas of functioning.'[31] Wilhelm Stekel— Sigmund Freud's 'apostle'—coined the term paraphilia in 1920; and sexologist John Money, author of *Venuses Penuses: Sexology, Sexosophy, and Exigency Theory* (1986), *Vandalized Lovemaps: Paraphilic Outcome of 7 Cases in Pediatric Sexology* (1989) *The Breathless Orgasm: A Lovemap Biography of Asphyxiophilia* (1991) and *Reinterpreting the Unspeakable: Human Sexuality 2000* (1994) popularized the term.

Michel Foucault has argued that it is the multiplicity of our sexual practices that constitute sex; that is, our formative sex lives comprise a complexity of habits, obsession, fantasies, and fetishes. 'Sexuality must not be thought of as a kind of natural given which power tries to hold in check, or as an obscure domain which knowledge tries gradually to uncover. It is the name that can be given to a historical construct: not a furtive reality that is difficult to grasp, but a great surface network in which the stimulation of bodies, the intensification of pleasures, the incitement to discourse, the formation of special knowledges, the strengthening of controls and resistances, are linked to one another, in accordance with a few major strategies of knowledge and power.'[32]

The hierarchy of habit, in some cases, leads to paraphilia. Sexual habits: one might prefer oral sex in preparation for orgasm rather than full intercourse. Some prefer intercourse in the missionary position, some reverse cowgirl. A narrative representation of this is enacted in the majority of pornographic films: kissing, undressing, breast fondling, masturbation of the female, masturbation of the male, oral sex with female, oral sex with male, missionary position, cowgirl, reverse cowgirl, doggy-style, anal missionary, anal cowgirl, anal reverse-cowgirl, anal doggy-style, exterior male orgasm. The transferability of desire from a living sexual partner to a corpse is a progression of perversity. A redetermination—recombination—of molecules appears normal. 'Yes, all becomings are molecular: the animal, flower or stone one becomes are molecular collectivities, haecceities, not molar subjects, objects, or form that we know from the outside and recognize through experience, through science, or by habit.[33] These perverse progressions, these narrative sexual successions show formalized habits apparent (with variations) in most pornographic movies. The final act—the male orgasm—is closure, the secession of habit. 'Habits are the very stuff our identities are made of. In them, we enact and thus define what we effectively are as social beings, often in contrast with our perception of what we are.'[34] Or as Jo Nesbø's Harry Hole would argue, 'There is a pattern. There's always a pattern. Not because you plan it, but because all humans are creatures of habit, there's no difference between you and me and the rapist.'[35]

Replacing Žižek's 'social' with 'sexual' creates obsession, the next stage in the hierarchy of habit. In recent years, the celebrity-obsessed stalker has become a media stock villain. However, the

most common form of stalking divides into two main classifications—psychotic and non-psychotic—and five sub-groups:
'Rejected stalkers pursue their victims in order to reverse,
correct, or avenge a rejection (e.g. divorce, separation, termi-
nation). Resentful stalkers pursue a vendetta because of a sense
of grievance against the victims—motivated mainly by the desire
to frighten and distress the victim. Intimacy seekers seek to
establish an intimate, loving relationship with their victim. To
them, the victim is a long-sought-after soul mate, and they were
'meant' to be together. Incompetent suitors, despite poor social
or courting skills, have a fixation, or in some cases a sense of
entitlement to an intimate relationship with those who have
attracted their amorous interest. Their victims are most often
already in a dating relationship with someone else. Predatory
stalkers spy on the victim in order to prepare and plan an
attack—usually sexual—on the victim.'[36] Only the predatory
stalker is psychotic and obsessed with sex—Sergeant Bertrand
fits into this category. But sexual obsession takes other forms.
Sexual obsession is a form of obsessive compulsive disorder in
which the person obsesses either about a person, his/her
sexuality, or a means by which he/she achieves sexual gratification—a ritualized habit to distinguish it from fantasy—fabricated habit. Person 'A' may be obsessed with Japanese women.
'B' with hairy, overweight men. 'C' with seamed stockings. 'D'
with studded butt plugs. The ritualized habit is a means towards
orgasm but not the sole means. Habit plus obsession leads us to
a Balkanization of sex within the pornographic industry—films
and magazines that cater for many different needs: women over
50, hairy men, dwarves, ladyboys, redheads, Asian girls, twinks,
BDSM, etc. Fantasy, then, becomes another component in the
hierarchy of habit.

A sexual fantasy or erotic fantasy (fictionalized habit) as a
means of heightening sexual feelings; an eroticized mental image
or scenario used for a number of reasons—to pass the time, to

achieve erection in men or vaginal-clitoral arousal in women, or to achieve orgasm. It may be a refiguration in the mind of past events—memerotic—or as wish-fulfilment projection. The fantasy itself need not be reified, in fact, most fantasies move towards a taboo subject/ action—paedophilia, rape, group sex, bondage. They can be prosaic fantasies: sex with the milkman (now pool boy), sex slave of Mr Darcy, aliens, or octopuses—as in Katsushika Hokusai's famous shunga *The Dream of the Fisherman's Wife* (circa 1820). Fantasies are also solitary pursuits, aids to masturbation. Mental role-playing that may lead to future erotic actualities. In Vladimir Nabokov's *Despair* a man watches his wife in the bedroom while fantasizing about watching himself having sex with his wife in the bedroom while watching the act—a sort of Quaker Oats box of fantasy and voyeurism. One might fantasize about one's work colleagues, people who share our morning or afternoon commute, schoolteachers, schoolgirls, nurses, doctors, plumbers; one may fantasize about having a 12-inch cock, a threesome with members of the Wu-Tang Clan, of being tied up and abused, there is no limit to the sexual imagination—but it is a mental image or a mental narrative not an actual act, it is an act of an act. For the actual, we need to move on from habit to obsession to fantasy to fetishism. 'As Hegel was already aware, there is something violent in the very symbolization of a thing, which equals its mortification. This violence operates at multiple levels. Language simplifies a designated thing, reducing it to a single feature. It dismembers the thing, destroying its organic unity, treating its parts and properties as autonomous. It inserts the thing into a field of meaning which is ultimately external to it.'[37] 'They were just men—and women, very occasionally—who did unacceptable things, as a factor of neurotic obsession. It was not a binary of good or evil, but a spectrum also inhabited by people who had to check their locks ten times at night, or who could not rest until the kitchen was tidy after each meal.'[38]

A fetish is an object-representation of a god, spirit, or super-natural being—a metonym for the thing worshipped. Present in all religions—the crucifix being a fetish object representing Christ and the Christian church—a fetish is an object believed to have supernatural properties. Likewise, a sexual fetish is an object representing the body as a whole that has replaced the body-as-a-whole. Alfred Binet in an article 'Le fetishisme dans l'amour' (Fetishism in love) in *Revue Philosophie*, 24, pp. 143–167 (1887) first used 'fetish' in its sexual connotation. Unlike habit, sexual fantasy, and sexual obsession, fetishism is classified as a mental disorder and a disease. Binet characterized two forms of fetishism 'spiritual love': an extreme form of obsession and fantasy involving social roles, occupations, etc.—see nurse outfits, maids, secretaries, etc.—and 'plastic love': a devotion to an object, phenomena or body part. The fetishism of body parts is technically termed 'partialism' foot fetish, etc., in this the body part replaces the genitals which in turn replace the body-as-a-whole. A fetish sexually arouses the individual and, in certain cases, may be the individual's primary means of orgasm. 'In this case, taken from Koester's scenario of Talbot's death, the injuries seem to have been sustained in an optimized auto-fatality, conceived by the driver as some kind of bizarre crucifixion. He would be mounted in the crash in an obscene position as if taking part in some grotesque act of intercourse—Christ crucified on the sodomized body of his own mother.'[39]

Sigmund Freud's analysis of fetishism centres on deprivation and castration:

'When now I announce that the fetish is a substitute for the penis, I shall certainly create disappointment; so I hasten to add that it is not a substitute for any chance penis, but for a particular and quite special penis that had been extremely important in early child-hood but had later been lost. That is to say, it should normally have been given up, but the fetish is precisely designed to preserve it from extinction. To put it more plainly: the fetish is a substitute for the woman's (the mother's) penis that the little boy once believed in and—for reasons familiar to us—does not want to give up.'[40]

Whether by association, deprivation and fear of the primary object's castration, or by conditioning and fixation, sexual fetishists come in three categories:

Objective fetishists—an object (a shoe, stockings, panties) replaces both physically and symbolically the desired other. Somatic fetishists—body parts (partialism) in which a foot, hand, finger, mouth becomes a metonym for the desired body (other). Its extreme form may be seen in the tradition of foot-binding in China or in the ankle-fetishism of Victorian Britain. Abstract fetishists, or pathological narcissism whereby the subject fetishizes an other's physical imperfections—amputations, obesity, unconsciousness—to emphasize the subject's perfection. Fetishism may begin in early childhood, a moment when phenomena replace and represent the primary object (mother caregiver) or as signifiers of the primary object—shoes, stockings. Most fetish objects are mirror similes of genitalia and body parts used in sex—shoes, boots, and gloves replace vaginas, penises, hands; while bondage masks and outfits emphasize genitalia or cover (absence as super-presence) desired areas. The materials of fetishism—leather, rubber, latex, fur, silk—mimic the desired skin, the skin (the primary object) forever absent. In transvestic fetishism (a form of objective-somatic fetishism), the clothes represent the absent primary object.

'The point of subjectification is the origin of the passional line of the postsignifying regime. The point of subjectification can be anything. It must only display the following characteristic traits of the subjective semiotic: the double turning away, betrayal, and existence under reprieve. For anorexics, food plays this role (anorexics do not confront death but save themselves by betraying food, which is equally a traitor since it is suspected of containing larvae, worms, and microbes). A dress, an article of underwear, a shoe are points of subjectification for a fetishist. So is a faciality trait for someone in love, but the meaning of faciality has changed; it is no longer the body of the signifier but has become the point of departure for a deterritorialization that puts everything else to flight. A thing, an animal, will do the trick. There are cogitos on everything. "A pair of eyes set far apart, a head hewn of quartz, a haunch that seemed to live its own life... Whenever the beauty of the female becomes irresistible, it is traceable to a single quality."'[41]

Richard von Krafft-Ebing (1840-1902) theorized that fetishism is pathological in nature, in that a sexual fetish (which should disappear like other childhood obsessions and fantasies) remains throughout a lifetime. '...the automobile, and in particular the automobile crash, provides a focus for the conceptualizing of a wide range of impulses involving the elements of psychopathology, sexuality, and self-sacrifice.'[42] Alfred Binet (1857-1911) argued that association is the primary reason for a fetish to occur, that sexual arousal happens accidentally in association with an object and that object—like Proust's mnemonic Madeleine—becomes intimately connected with sexual excitement and orgasm—what he terms 'l'amour plastique'. Havelock Ellis (1859-1939) asserted that we are sexual beings at a very early age and that children's primary sexual arousal defines their sexuality. 'We wish to make a simple point about psycho-analysis: from the beginning, it has often encountered the question of the becomings-animal of the human being: in children, who continually undergo becomings of this kind; in fetishism and in particular masochism, which continually confront this problem. The least that can be said is that the psychoanalysts, even Jung, did not understand, or did not want to understand. They killed becoming-animal, in the adult as in the child.'[43] Magnus Hirschfeld (1868-1935) believed all of us to be fetishists but that an over-emphasis on a certain object creates a pathological fetishism. Thumb-sucking, cuddly toys and pacifiers are all transitional objects. Donald Winnicott (1896-1971) stated, 'Fetish can be described in terms of a persistence of a specific object or type of object dating from infantile experience in the transitional field, linked with the delusion of a maternal phallus,' and 'a specific object or type of object, dating from an experience during the period where the mother gradually pulls back as an immediate provider of satisfaction of the child's desires, persists as a characteristic in adult sexual life.'[44] *The International Statistical Classification of Diseases and Related Health Problems*, published by the World Health Organization in 2005, classifies fetishism as 'the use of inanimate objects as a stimulus to achieve sexual arousal and satisfaction; in most cases said object is required for sexual gratification.' *The American Psychiatric Association's Diagnostic and Statistical Manual of Mental Disorders* (2000) categorizes fetishism as 'the use of nonliving objects as a stimulus to achieve sexual arousal or satisfaction. (This only applies if the objects are not specifically designed for sexual stimulation (e.g., a vibrator)).'

'The head, even the human head, is not necessarily a face. The face is produced only when the head ceases to be a part of the body, when it ceases to be coded by the body, when it ceases to have a multidimensional, polyvocal corporeal code—when the body, head included, has been decoded and has to be overcoded by something we shall call the Face. This amounts to saying that the head, all the volume-cavity elements of the head, have to be facialized. What accomplishes this is the screen with holes, the white wall/ black hole, the abstract machine producing faciality. But the operation does not end there: if the head and its elements are facialized, the entire body also can be facialized, comes to be facialized as part of an inevitable process. When the mouth and nose, but first the eyes, become a holey surface, all the other volumes and cavities of the body follow. An operation worthy of Doctor Moreau: horrible and magnificent. Hand, breast, stomach, penis and vagina, thigh, leg and foot, all come to be facialized.

Fetishism, erotomania, etc., are inseparable from these processes of facialization. It is not at all a question of taking a part of the body and making it resemble a face, or making a dream-face dance in a cloud. No anthropomorphism here. Facialization operates not by resemblance but by an order of reasons. It is a much more unconscious and machinic operation that draws the entire body across the holey surface, and in which the role of the face is not as a model or image, but as an overcoding of all of the decoded parts. Everything remains sexual; there is no sublimation, but there are new coordinates.'[45] Hans Bellmer meets J.G. Ballard meets Sergeant Bertrand in a re-assembled body that resembles the human but is a fetishization of the anthropomorphic, a metonymous construction of the living dead.

Did Sergeant Bertrand's mother die when he was a young child and her inanimate body become phenomena replacing the primary object? Was he exposed to her body, the dead body becoming the object, the fetish of his awakening sexuality? A mourning room filled with aunts, fussing around the body, powdering its face, making it beautiful? But not all who see dead mothers turn into Norman Bates, turn into Sergeant Bertrand. One could argue that the dead body, the object of the necrophile's sexual obsession, is an inanimate, nonliving possession, used to achieve sexual fulfilment, no different from a shoe. Why, then, is the event of necrophilia so abhorrent and how did the good soldier Bertrand become the precursor of those twentieth-century ghouls Ted Bundy and Jeffrey Dahmer? 'This is why Oedipus gathers up everything, everything is found again in Oedipus, which is indeed the result of universal history, but in the singular sense in which capital is already the result. Fetishes, idols, images, and simulacra—here we have the whole series: territorial fetishes, despotic idols or symbols, then everything is recapitulated in the images of capitalism, which shapes and reduces them to Oedipal simulacrum.'[46]

Is necrophilia a fetish? Or is it a mania? What is it that drives a man to violate a dead body in order to achieve (for him) the ultimate orgasm? Is it any more shocking than other forms of paraphilia? In *Necrophilia: Forensic and Medico-Legal Aspects*, Anil Aggrawal calls for a new classification of necrophilia, critiquing previous classifications and setting out ten separate classes of necrophiliac behaviour. In 1886, Krafft-Ebing classified necrophiles in two categories—ones who used corpses for sexual purposes—so passive necrophiles, and active necrophiles who killed out of desire for sex with a dead body and mutilated them in the process. Erich Wulffen added a further category in 1910, in addition to lust murder (necrosadism), and having sex with an already dead body (necrostuprum), he added necrophagy involving consumption of dead flesh. In 1931, Ernest Jones argued that passive necrophilia—sex with an already dead body—fell into two categories: sex with a loved one (partner, relative) and sex with a non-loved one's corpse—both involving extreme forms of masochism and sadism. Magnus Hirschfield claimed something similar to Krafft-Ebing, stating that necrophiles either sexually abused corpses or that they murdered in order to destroy the person and then further humiliate the body through sex. Thirty years later, J. Rosman and P. Resnick Rosman concluded that necrophiles fell into two groups— genuine necrophiles and pseudonecrophiles. Genuine necrophiles are sexually attracted to corpses and include the three subgroups of necrophiliac homicides, regular necrophiles who use bodies for sex, and a group who use necrophiliac fantasy as a sexual release without having contact with an actual corpse. Aggrawal suggest an extension of these classifications due to the increase in information on necrophiles.[47]

Class I—'role players,' such as the Austrian incestuous rapist Josef Fritzl, who do not desire sex with a corpse but prefer their sexual partner (however coerced) to be utterly passive, feigning death. Class II—'romantic necrophiles' who keep a body or body part of a loved one in order to continue having sex with their partner. Class III—'necrophiliac fantasizers'—those who create sexual fantasies involving a corpse, masturbate in cemeteries, etc. Class IV—'tactile necrophiles' who like to touch corpses and masturbate over them. 'Fetishistic necrophiles' make up Class V—use body parts as sexual fetishes. Class VI involves 'necro-mutilomaniacs' who achieve sexual orgasm through mutilation of corpses—Sergeant Bertrand was a necromutilomaniac. Morturay attendants, gravediggers, medical workers and alike fall into Class VII—'Opportunistic necrophiles'—those who have sex with living partners but when able will take the opportunity to fuck dead bodies. Class VIII—'regular necrophiles' who have sex with dead bodies, haunters of graveyards, morgues, these 'regular necrophiles' are able to have sex with the living and will not kill to satiate their lust; that falls to those in Class IX, the 'homicidal necrophiles' who murder and mutilate in order to have sex with a dead body or as a means of controlling that body (see Jeffrey Dahmer and Dennis Nilsen) but can also have sex with a living person. Finally, Class X necrophiles who can only be sexually stimulated by having intercourse (orally, anally, vaginally, or in any created orifice) with a dead body.

Although there are crossovers and anomalies in Aggrawal's studies, this new classification extends Krafft-Ebing's basic dual categorization and provides a basis for an investigation into the different forms of necrophilia. Aggrawal's legal and medical research also looks into the aetiology and epidemiology of necrophilia, which complements the categories and sexual studies.[48]

The aetiology of necrophilia is murky, confusing, and rests on theoretical assumptions and propositional analysis. Although Havelock Ellis[49] suggested a congenital defect as a basis for necrophilia in the case of a gravedigger who suffered from anosmia (inability to perceive odours) and whose mother was highly sexed. Ellis argues that because the man thought the act of necrophilia normal—and that he lacked the sense of smell—

then his acts were caused by congenital defects, blaming the man's mother, her sexual proclivities, and lack of intelligence for her son's necrophilia—if this categorization were applied to the general populace, it would mean necrophilia was more prevalent than studies suggest. Brill[50] argues that heredity could play a part in the emergence of necrophiliac tendencies, documenting a man whose aggressive and criminalistic father and psychologically feeble mother caused him to be effeminate, this, Brill claims, mixed with an oral fixation resulted in necrophiliac acts. 'But Christie had frightened her. Although Mrs Christie wasn't there, he had done some strange intimate things, asked her to open her mouth so he could look down her throat with a mirror on the end of a rod, and asked her to lift her skirt up to mid-thigh level.'[51] Case studies cite trauma as a potential cause, head injuries causing a shift in sexuality and attendant aggression causing a desire for sex with dead bodies—see below the cases of John Reginald Halliday Christie and Fred West for possible trauma-induced aetiology. In Christie's case, sexual inadequacy may also have been a cause—Christie had a very small penis and felt inadequate when confronted by living women, preferring them to either play dead or be dead before he had sex with them. Alcoholism and drug use may be contributing factors, see below Jeffrey Dahmer and Dennis Nilsen as examples of homosexual necrophiles who used alcohol and drugs to not only embolden themselves but to incapacitate their victims. 'His body went rigid. He grabbed my jumper with both hands, shouting inarticulately. Hot bright pain shot through my chest as Dr Drummond's incision came open again. I sliced at Sam's fingers, felt the blade scrape across bone. He made an awful sound halfway between a sob and a scream. I imagined him trying to comprehend what was happening through his alcoholic haze, and I cursed myself for drinking enough to make me clumsy. I'd meant to send him off quick and clean. This was no better than butchery.'[52] Temporal lobe anomalies—severe headaches, hallucinations, sometimes caused by alcohol and drugs—are evident in paraphilias such as necrophilia. Poe's use of opium may have fuelled his necrophiliac stories: 'And again I sunk into visions of Ligeia—and again, (what marvel that I shudder while I write,) again there reached my ears a low sob from the region of the ebony bed. But why shall I minutely detail the unspeakable horrors of that night? Why shall I pause to relate how, time after time, until near the period of the gray dawn, this hideous drama of revivification was repeated; how each terrific relapse was only into a sterner and apparently more irredeemable death; how each agony wore the aspect of a struggle with some invisible foe; and how each struggle was succeeded by I know not what of wild change in the personal appearance of the corpse?'[53] Aggrawal cites harsh treatment, excessive criticism, and childhood neglect as contributory factors; and Ted Bundy, Fred West, and other necrophiles suffered from one or all of these, yet so have a large number of children. Fred West also suffered sexual abuse in childhood, another possible cause of necrophiliac tendencies. Some or all of these aetiologies may combine to create a personality disorder[54] that results in a desire for the dead; but, I would argue, in the majority of cases does not. Theories as to the cause of necrophilia range from congenital deficiency, feeble-mindedness, mental weakness, to neo-Freudian analysis of childhood, dreams, and language, viewing necrophilia as a revenge sexual act on the displaced and transferred body of the mother—see the later analysis of Jerry Brudos.

There is also a question of power and possession, the body relegated to that of sexual slave and passive object used and abused, fucked and discarded—an element of role playing and sadomasochism, not wholly connected with necrophilia—but taken to its extreme, it results in lust murderers like Dennis Nilsen and Gary Ridgway. Conversely, lack of control may ignite violence and result in the passive victim enacting revenge: as in the case of a 16-year-old student who killed his mother after years of forced incest and then anally and vaginally raped her dead body. Fear of castration, an ongoing infantile sexuality, narcissism, and the Oedipus complex have all been cited as factors in the psychology of necrophiles and so have mourning, obsessive love, opportunism and rejection by a partner. No single cause creates a necrophile. All of the above may contribute to a desire to have sex with dead bodies—Bertrand himself was a narcissist with a possible Oedipal complex who may have suffered head trauma and hallucinations. If this is the case, then how widespread is necrophilia? Aggrwaal provides an epidemiological overview.[55]

As the aetiology of necrophilia shows, the contributing factors that cause a sexual desire for the dead could also create other paraphilias, or none at all. As Aggrawal points out, necrophilia is possibly the most secret of acts with the partner/ victim forever silent. Is necrophilia more widespread than reports and studies show? As necrophilia was not until recently considered a crime, then the lack of reporting on the subject is understandable—it can be argued that it is a victimless crime, but then one could argue that it is a crime against property if the family or religious denomination claim the body as their own. Aggrawal uses Rosman and Resnick's 'Sexual attraction to corpses: a psychiatric review of necrophilia'[56] as the basis of an epidemiology and as character analysis. Out of a study of 122 necrophiles, they found an age range from 16 to 65—a normal range for sexually active men and women of all persuasions. 95% of these were men, 14 of whom had committed murder for necrophiliac purposes. Intelligence levels across the group ranged from signs of insanity to those with a high IQ (the means of assessment). Heterosexuality, bisexuality, and homosexuality in necrophiles corresponded to statistical evidence in society. Alcohol and drug use may contribute to necrophiliac acts, however Rosman and Resnick's analysis failed to find evidence in the reports they analyzed. Sex of corpse—10% of necrophiles chose same-sex corpses, this statistic was higher—50%—among necrophiliac killers. Marital status—60% single, 26% married, and 14% divorced or widowed. A large percentage of all necrophiles showed a prior tendency towards sadism and cruelty. The survey found no evidence that psychotics, people suffering personality disorders, or having unusual belief systems, made up a large proportion of the group. Occupation—although Rosman and Resnick found evidence that hospital orderlies, cemetery employees, morgue attendants, funeral parlour assistants, soldiers, clerics, pathologists, anatomy students, ambulance drivers, and volunteer firemen had all been found to have a predilection for sex with corpses it was not stated whether the necrophilia was a result of opportunity—all professions having access to corpses—or that the person had manoeuvred themself into a job in which they had access to the objects of their desire.[57] Helpful as the aetiology and epidemiology are, neither provides any firm conclusions as to the cause or profusion of necrophilia in history and society. 'He needs to do it so much and knows that he can't live without it—and in any event, no matter how hard he tries, he's already done it and there can never be any real peace or any hope of forgiveness. His life is tainted and he can't go back.[58]

3

NecroHysteria — A Short History

Describing Egyptian embalming methods in *The History*, circa 440 BCE, Herodotus writes, 'The wives of distinguished men, when they die, they do not give for embalmment right away, nor yet women who are especially beautiful and of great account. Only when they have been dead three or four days do they hand them over to the embalmers. This is done to prevent the embalmers from copulating with these women. For they say that one of them was caught copulating with a freshly dead woman and that a fellow workman told on him.'[59] In the 1940s, Ed Gein would wait at least three or four days before disinterring a woman's corpse (or part of) for whatever sexual purpose he had in mind. 2,500 years before Gein's crimes were unearthed, Herodotus describes the prevalence of similar taboos of necrophilia in Ancient Egypt.

There are necrophiles who only experience full sexual satis-faction from having sex with a dead body, and there are those that copulate with corpses because of their availability and the unavailability (or impossibility) of having sex with a living person. Is it a freedom of sexual choice or a weakness and failing of the super-ego? From the time of the pre-Socratic philosopher Empedocles (490-430 BCE), who 'kept a woman alive for thirty days without breath or pulse,'[60] to the library of books on serial killers and sex murderers, writers and historians have been fasci-nated with necrophiles and necrophilia. 'Before I began killing boys, and afterward when I couldn't find one or hadn't the energy to go looking, there was another thing I would sometimes do. It began as a crude masturbation technique and ended very near mysticism. At the trial they called me necrophiliac without considering the ancient roots of the word, or its profound resonance. I was friend of the dead, lover of the dead. And I was my own first friend and lover.'[61]

If '[d]eath is the last great taboo,' if '[w]e cannot look it in the face for fear of seeing the skull beneath the skin,'[62] surely having sex with a dead body, penetrating that skull beneath the deliquescing flesh, is the greater taboo, and the one from which to begin to philosophize about the human condition. Referring back to Herodotus and forward 2,000 years to Montaigne's moral epigram formulated from his thoughts on Egyptian death rites in which he states he has 'formed the habit of having death continually present, not merely in my imagination, but in my mouth,'[63] then the occurrence of necrophilia among Egyptian embalmers through to the likes of Ed Gein, Ted Bundy, and Jeffrey Dahmer shows that death and the love of the dead is not merely a myth, not part of our dark imaginings, but part of human culture, continually present, a parallel world in which love turns into pathological obsession and a close proximity to death becomes a perversion. 'Then he turned to the girl. He took off all her clothes and looked at her, inspecting her body carefully, as if he would see how she were made. He went outside and looked in through the window at her lying naked before the fire. When he came back in he unbuckled his trousers and stepped out of them and laid next to her. He pulled the blanket over them.'[64]

In 1931, Carl von Cosel (Carl Tanzer), a radiologist and amateur inventor in his mid-50s, took an obsessive interest in 22-year-old Maria Elena Milagro de Hoyos, a tuberculosis patient at the sanitarium in which he worked in Key West, Florida. After falling in love with the attractive woman, he bought her jewellery and other gifts, and used his medical knowledge to try to cure her, but Elena succumbed to her illness and died in October of that year. Distraught, von Cosel had a mausoleum constructed in Key West Cemetery in which—with the consent of her family—he preserved her body in formaldehyde. He would visit her and talk to her, installing a telephone so he could speak to her at all times. But even that was not enough—it did not dampen his obsession or his desire. Two years after he first fell in love, he disentombed the embalmed body and took it home on a pushcart. 'Decay had set in in a most disheartening manner. Only with the greatest care was I able to peel the pieces of textile from the body; this took hours. We then lifted the body out of the coffin and laid it on a table with a clean sheet. Having sprayed the body all over again, I now proceeded to sponge her, face with a specially prepared solution and also her hands and feet. With dismay I discovered that in view of the damage already done much more cleaning was required than could be done in the one night I had the morgue at my disposal.'[65] He rigged her bones with piano wire and coat hangers, inserted glass eyes into the orbital sockets when her real eyes putrefied, smothered her with wax and make-up, replaced some of her rotting skin with silk, had a wig fashioned, eviscerated the body and filled it with rags like a Guy Fawkes dummy, and dressed her (it) as a bride. To enable sexual congress with Elena, he intruded a paper tube into what was once her vagina. 'Long I lay thus, holding her closely to me, the living and the dead united in love. The sweetness, of this was divine. Never had I dreamt that she had preserved so sweet and intense a love for me after being in the grave so long. Was it possible? I could hardly grasp or believe it, but here was the undeniable evidence. Life and death united together, eye to eye.'[66] As David Foster Wallace has pointed out in *Both Flesh And Not*, 'the unpleasant is perfectly OK, just so long as it rivets.'[67] Von Cosel lived with his corpse bride for seven years before Elena's sister—acting on information—discovered the body in his house and reported him to the police. A local rest home put his lover's body on public display. Von Cosel underwent psychiatric tests in prison while awaiting trial but the case never made it to court. Authorities reburied the corpse in an unmarked grave. Von Cosel responded by making a life-size doll of Elena, incorporating her death mask, and lived with it until he died in 1952. Von Cosel's necrophilia attracted attention in the news and the arts, and horror writers used his actions as building blocks for shocking tales of tomb raiding and lust, murder and eroticism, madness and pornography.[68]

Von Cosel's necrophilia centred on one corpse on/in whom/ which he consummated his possessive love regardless of societal norms. He transgressed any repressive balance, any primary principles. 'I had begun feeding her body orally with nourishing fluids regularly every day.'[69] The object transference of his libido from dying woman to dead body enacts the 'limitlessness in desire,'[70] where 'urges of the flesh pass all bounds in the absence of controlling will.'[71] The id (the duality of the libido and the death drive) overwhelms the super-ego. As Freud has it, 'Each one of us goes a bit too far, either here or there, in transgressing the boundaries that we have drawn up in our sexual lives. The perversions are neither bestialities nor degeneracies in the dramatic sense of that word. They are the development of germs that are all contained within the undifferentiated sexual predis-position of a child, the suppression of which or their application to higher, asexual goals—their sublimation—is destined to supply the forces behind a large number of our cultural achieve-ments. So if someone has become coarse and manifestly perverse, it would be more accurate to say that he has remained so, that he represents a stage of an arrested development.'[72]

If von Cosel's obsessive love became necrophilia, then the following case is an example of proximal desire for the dead. Women are not adverse to corpse love. Karen Greenlee, who worked in the funeral business, had an overwhelming desire for men in their twenties and thirties—dead men in their twenties and thirties. One day in 1979, driving a hearse from Sacramento Memorial Lawn Mortuary to a nearby cemetery containing the coffin and body of John Mercure, a 33-year-old male, Greenlee made a detour, taking the corpse back to her house to act out her codeine-fuelled sexual fantasies. After two days, the authorities tracked her down and arrested her. In the dead man's coffin, police found a four-page note revealing her necro-erotic exploits with between 20 and 40 dead bodies. Remorseful, she questioned her motives, asking if her fear of love had turned into a love of death, calling herself a 'morgue rat,' and categorizing her desire as 'a rathole, perhaps my grave.'[73] As California had no law against necrophilia until 10 September 2004, the court fined Greenlee $225 and jailed her for eleven days for car theft and misdemeanours pertaining to the illegal removal of a corpse. On her release, as part of the terms of her two-year probation, Greenlee agreed to undergo psychiatric assessments. The corpses satisfied her sexual need not through penetration but by clitoral stimulation and frottage, while the attendant cold touch and embalming-fluid aroma of the dead body gratified the necro-mantic ritual of burial and the stimulant rush of taboo. She would arrive at night, use her keys to the funeral home, and spend hours riding the bodies cowgirl style, the dead men would have their own orgasm, spilling a little blood from their mouths. She would even attend the funerals, her gasps and cries erotic simulations of grief. From an early age, she had been attracted to death; she had her own pet cemetery, and became obsessed with the local funeral home, wandering its corridors, stealing into its chapels. When bodies were not available in her place of work, she broke into other funeral homes, sometimes into tombs—as long as the men were between 20 and 40 and were not fat, she felt attracted to them, whether or not they had died in car crashes, had been shot, or had self-asphyxiated in an auto-erotic accident.

The first scene of *Nekromantik 2* shows Robert Schmadtke from Nekromantik[74] killing himself. A woman, Monika, disinters his body and takes it home. She attempts to have sex with Rob's body but cannot reach orgasm. Monika then meets up with a man called Mark to watch a movie—which shows a very Bataillean scene of naked people eating boiled eggs. Attracted to Mark, Monika now wants to get rid of Rob's corpse, so she cuts it up and keeps a few mementoes—his penis and head. But sex with the living Mark does not satisfy her and Mark starts to have doubts about the relationship after finding Rob's castrated penis in the refrigerator. Returning to the apartment with a pizza to witness Monika and her friends watching a documentary about an autopsy on a seal, Mark finds the film disgusting. The couple argue and Mark leaves. After a telephone conversation, they get together and have sex, Monika on top trying to prevent Mark moving in order to simulate her necrosexual fantasies. Then, unsatisfied by the role-playing, Monika grabs a saw she has hidden under the bed and thrusts it into Mark's neck. As he is about to be decapitated, she takes out a cock ring and places it on his still erect penis. Monika then puts Mark's decapitated head on Rob's corpse's shoulders. 'At last, one day at six, when the oblique sunshine was directly lighting the bathroom, a half sucked egg was suddenly invaded by the water, and after filling up with a bizarre noise, it was shipwrecked before our very eyes. This incident was so extraordinarily meaningful to Simone that her body tautened and she had a long climax, virtually drinking my left eye between her lips. Then, without leaving the eye, which was sucked as obstinately as a breast, she sat down, wrenching my head toward her on the seat, and she pissed noisily on the bobbing eggs with total vigor and satisfaction.'[75]

Although female necrophiles are rare, they do exist, most having a morbid fascination with death and an erotic inclination to the material of death. In 2012, a 37-year-old woman in Sweden was arrested and charged with having sexual contact with a human skeleton. Investigators discovered human bones, skulls at her apartment in Gothenburg along with CDs with titles such as *My First Experience* and *My Necrophilia* which contained images of the woman using a skeleton for sexual purposes, a practice that the police described as "unethical". The skeleton was found to be at least 50 years old, and she had purchased the assortment of bones over the internet. The woman's obsession with death, she also collected images of morgues and cemeteries, became so intense that she needed to fulfil her desire to experience necrophilia albeit with a skeleton rather than a corpse.

Obsessive love and erotic proximity must still surmount the mucky reality of a dead body, as Freud notes, 'One would be inclined to see disgust as one of the powers which have imposed boundaries upon the sexual goal … The strength of the sexual drive enjoys actively overcoming disgust.'[76] Taboos are cultural indicators, inhibitors, operating and shuttling between the sacred and the uncanny, the religious and the unclean, the spirit and the body, the metaphysical and the sexual; base boundaries of the Judeo-Christian moral and ethical system. 'You shall not'—a Decalogue of taboos defining human actions and events, instrumental in forming individual conscience and societal morality.[77] For some civilizations, boundaries collapse, a taboo becomes a fetish, the unclean object transformed and transferred from disgust to desire, the individual perversion becomes a societal one, the transgressor escapes punishment, the crime transmutes into custom, the prohibited is apotheosized.

From the first until the eighth century CE, the Moche people of the northern Peruvian coast fashioned jewellery and ceramics, built pyramids and farms, their technology incorporated sophisticated irrigation systems and weaving methods, and they based their religion on human sacrifice and ritual cannibalism. When archaeologists in the 1990s excavated *Huaca de la Luna* (Pyramid of the Moon) and *Huaca del Sol* (Pyramid of the Sun), they found murals showing a horrifying multi-limbed and many-fanged god whom they dubbed the Decapitator, plus pottery depicting horrific scenes of war, death, and sex—sometimes all three. There were also images of Moche priests slitting throats, the gouts of blood collected in bowls and imbibed, living people and excarnated bodies copulating in a fleshed and defleshed orgiastic ritual, several pots show a woman masturbating a skeleton. The Moche used this ritualistic necrophilia as a means of fertility-rite time travel, procreation in time and space, where 'the context of the tomb puts sex into the house of the dead, expanding reproductive time far back into the past-and forward toward the future.'[78] The pots depict anal wormholes (vaginal sex is rarely depicted) of desire and death, procreation and annihilation in which disgust is eradicated, made sacred, and masturbating corpses are used as a means of transferring bodily fluids, transforming death, the skeleton's semen holding the life force that transgresses the human body in its corporeal form. Likewise, in sixteenth-century Europe, Hans Baldung Grien's painting *Death and Woman* (1518-20) and Niklaus Manuel Deutsch *Death and the Maiden* (1517) and his *Dance of Death* fresco in Berne (1516-19) all depict women consorting with skeletons.

1200 years later, Marvel Comics' Jack Kirby created a supergod Thanos who 'courted Death itself in the alluring form of a robed, hooded, voluptuously breasted female figure,'[79] an erotic siren, a Playboy centrefold sporting the double-Ds of death and desire. In other Marvel Comics editions, Death appeared the instant before someone dies, taking the form of a lover. At Captain Marvel's death, it materialized as his greatest love Una (truth).

Returning to other superheroes and demigods, during the Trojan war (ca. 1194–1184 BCE), the Amazon warrior Penthesileia, seeking atonement after unintentionally killing her sister Hippolyte while firing an arrow at a stag they were hunting, vows to kill the Greek hero Achilles. After slaughtering many men, including Podarces, she comes to blows with Telemon Ajax before battling Achilles, the noble son of Peleus impaling her and her wind-swift horse with his host-destroying spear. As the bodies lie quivering in the dust, Achilles removes the Amazon's war helmet and is ensorcelled by the goddess-like beauty of the daughter of the war god Ares. Wishing he had taken her for his bride, he falls upon the body in remorse and lust, and later kills his fellow Achaean Thersites for calling him a 'perverted man.'[80]

Taken from an historical account by Phylarchus (third century BCE), Parthenius of Nicaea, the last of the Alexandrian poets, writes in his Erotica Pathemata (of the sorrows of love—circa first century BCE) of Dimoetes who married Evopis the daughter of his brother Troezen. But the girl loved another, her own brother. When Dimoetes discovered that the siblings were having sex, he told his brother. Terrified and stigmatized, the young girl put a noose around her neck and, damning Dimoetes, hanged herself. Maybe eroticized by the suicide, Dimoetes, walking along the beach, saw the body of an extremely beautiful woman roiling in the surf; he dashed in and pulled her to the shore. He fell in love with her and took the corpse back to his dwelling where his desire overwhelmed him and he had sex with the dead body. He kept her as long as he could, but the body began to deliquesce and disintegrate, and, finally, the putrescence became too much and he interred her in an opulent tomb. Even then, his passion would not abate and, his sexual obsession with a corpse undimmed, he killed himself with his own sword.[81]

Achilles, Dimoetes, and Carl von Cosel each honour their dead lovers with a magnificent burial, or build tombs for them—Achilles arranges for the ashes of his would-be corpse bride to be interred in King Laomedon's tomb within the walls of Ilium. These men fall under the classification of necromantics, obsessed with their love and desire for a singular loved one, rather than erotic compulsion to have sex with corpses, as in Karen Greenlee's case. However, in the building of tombs, Achilles, Dimoetes, and von Cosel transfer their desire to a spiritual communion with the dead—similar to Mochean culture, as a device to either disable time (von Cosel's rebuilding of his lover's body), or to reverse time (Achilles taking of the dreaded and warlike Penthesileia as his posthumous bride), or folding time and space as in Dimoetes's transubstantiation (sublimation) of his incestuous wife's hanging body with the drowned body he preserves.

Composed between the third and sixth centuries CE, the Babylonian Talmud accused King Herod the Great of necrophilia.[82] In 29 CE, after sentencing his second wife Mariamne the Hasmonean to death for alleged adultery and conspiracy to murder—an executioner strangled her with a silken cord—the repentant yet delirious and psychotic Herod had his beautiful dead wife embalmed in honey and stored in his palace for the next seven years. His sexual desire for his mellified wife remained as strong as when she was alive. The contemporary Judeo-Roman historian Titus Flavius Josephus states that, 'His love for Mariamne seemed to seize him in such a peculiar manner, as looked like Divine vengeance upon him for the taking away her life; for he would frequently call for her, and frequently lament for her in a most indecent manner.'[83] Herod even outdid Achilles, Dimoetes, and von Cosel by building the Mariamne Tower, a sumptuous fortress palace in Jerusalem, and one of only three buildings to survive the siege and destruction of Jerusalem by the future emperor Titus Flavius Vespasianus in 70 CE.

These edifices, these architectures of forbidden yet realized desire, these tomb/ wombs for an object already and always gone, are structures of anti-repression, fortresses of desire as a 'countereffect of lack.' If desire is the 'abject fear of lacking something,'[84] then the maintenance of the body, even if it is an inanimate vessel for sexual congress, is also an attempt to preserve and sustain the real, for 'if desire produces, its product is real. If desire is productive, it can be productive only in the real world and can produce only reality. Desire is the set of passive syntheses that engineer partial objects, flows, and bodies, and that function as units of production. The real is the end product, the result of the passive syntheses of desire as the autoproduction of the unconscious.'[85] The dead agents of desire were as real to the Moche, to Achilles, to Herod, to Dimoetes, to von Cosel as their priests, warriors, slaves, and fellow workers, they were products of the necrophile's reality, produced out of the flow of saliva over their dead bodies, the end product of semen within, the passive bodies synthesizing with the active functions of the partial objects—mouth, penis, testicles—of the living lovers, the architects of their sumptuous sarcophagi, their thanatic stone boudoir.

The Metaphysical poet Henry Vaughan (1622-1695) wrote:

Dear, beauteous Death! the jewel of the Just,
Shining nowhere, but in the dark;
What mysteries do lie beyond thy dust,
Could man outlook that mark![86]

His twin brother Thomas hints that he may have breached that mark, transgressing morality and religious teachings in the pursuit of magic. Thomas Vaughan, alchemist Kabbalist, Rosicrucian, and occultist explains in his essay 'Aqua vitae non vitis', 'On the same day my dear wife sickened, being a Friday, and at the same time of the day, namely in the evening, my gracious God did put into my heart the secret of extracting the oil of Halcali, which I had once accidentally found at the Pinner of Wakefield in the days of my most dear wife. But it was again taken from me by a most wonderful judgement of God, for I could never remember how I did it, but made a hundred attempts in vain. And now my glorious God (Whose name be praised for ever) has brought it again into my mind, and on the same day my dear wife sickened; and on the Saturday following, which was the day she died on, I extracted it by the former practice: so that on the same day, which proved the most sorrowful to me, whatever can be, God was pleased to confer upon me the greatest joy I can ever have in this world after her death.'[87]

The editor notes that the 'former practice' involved the 'dark fashion' of 'viscous and spermatic humidity'[88] in order to extract the 'menstruum universale'. The Metaphysical poets equated love with death, sex with decay, inspiration with expiration.

George Herbert's 'Mortification': 'That dumbe inclosure maketh love

/ Unto the coffin, that attends his death,' and in 'Death' Herbert believes death's 'bones with beauty shall be clad.' Donne, militantly positive, states in 'Death, be not proud' that from death 'Much pleasure; then from thee much more must flow, / And soonest our best men with thee do go,' in these poems there is an almost erotic sense of the presence of death, Marvell even invokes the terror of vermicular necrophiliac rape in an attempt to seduce his mistress.

> But at my back I always hear Time's winged chariot hurrying
> near:
> And yonder all before us lie
> Deserts of vast eternity.
> Thy beauty shall no more be found;
> Nor, in thy marble vaults, shall sound
> My echoing song; then worms shall try
> That long-preserved virginity,
> And your quaint honour turn to dust,
> And into ashes all my lust:
> The grave's a fine and private place,
> But none, I think, do there embrace.[89]

The American poet Kenneth Rexroth argued that Thomas Vaughan's mystical writings under the name 'Eugenius Philalethes' were exegeses on sexual methodology, particularly Tantric sex, in which the sexual fluids of the yogi and yogini cover the body of the initiate.

When the playwright William Congreve—author of *The Mourning Bride*—died in 1729, his mistress Henrietta Godolphin, 2nd Duchess of Marlborough, had a realistic mannequin made, dressed it in Congreve's clothes, fitted his death mask to it and slept with it, finally taking it to her grave in 1733. In the early eighteenth century, Sir John Price had his first wife's body embalmed and placed in his bed. He, his corpse, and his second wife slept together. When his second wife died and he, too, had her embalmed and placed next to his first corpse bride, his third wife politely asked if he would not mind burying the bodies, after all, there could not have been much room.

The Marquis de Sade's *Justine*, published in 1791, depicts various acts of necrophilia. After being split nearly in half by the engorged penis of a sexually-enraged donkey, a young woman, her intestines spilling out onto the floor, dies and her wound is penetrated by an onlooker while another licks the donkey's excrement-stained anus.[90] In *Juliette* (1797-1801), a father rapes his daughter's disinterred corpse and Juliette asks four men to sodomize her dead sister. In *The 120 days of Sodom* (1785), a man hires prostitutes and visits funeral parlours, standing over the coffins, he has the women masturbate him so that his semen splashes onto the dead bodies.[91] Another man sodomizes the body of a dead boy while kissing the buttocks of a dead girl. Yet another kills a woman while buggering her and then has vaginal sex with the body. A father copulates with his daughter while pretending she is dead. Corpses—fresh or putrid—are subjected to vaginal, anal, and oral sex, wounds are penetrated, and they are given enemas and raped with dildos. Foucault writes, 'In Sade, sex is without any norm or intrinsic rule that might be formulated from its own nature, but it is subject to the unrestricted law of a power which itself knows no other law but its own; if by chance it is at times forced to accept the order of progressions carefully disciplined into successive days, this exercise carries it to a point where it is no longer anything but a unique and naked sovereignty: an unlimited right of all-powerful monstrosity.'[92]

As Blanchot would have it, Sade resides in the 'anonymous tomb of his renown,'[93] his books are edifices of desire and death, his removed skull as psycho-scientifically studied as that of the

poisoned skull of Gloriana in Middleton / Tourneur's
necrophiliac *The Revenger's Tragedy*. Sade created the space of
transgression, the architecture of a will to desire where human
bones are used as dildos disregarding and destroying any laws
of nature, any divine interference, and royal proclamation, he
opened the 'uncanny abyss of freedom without any ontological
guarantee in the Order of Being.'[94] In Sade's works necrophiliac
'eroticism seems to derive from the transgressive and fetishistic
nature of the act rather than from a specific focus on the dead
body as a sexually arousing object ... necrophilia is a graphic
expression of the libertine's megalomania, in that the dead
body's utter defencelessness allows him to enact the fantasy of
total domination.'[95]

In the early 1860s, the British prime minister Lord Palmerston
and his ministers attempted to protect Queen Victoria from her
perceived 'necrophilia'.[96] The object of this (mis)perception, the
Albert Memorial—completed in 1872, ten years after the death of
Victoria's beloved Prince Consort—showed how the queen
'pushe(d) to the limit the realization of something that might be
called the pure and simple desire of death as such.'[97] She incar-
nated that desire in the elaborate Gothic structure standing 54m
tall. The statue of Albert seated beneath and within the tower,
transforms the memorial into a Gothic spaceship, Albert as pilot,
a steampunk version of Giger's Alien space jockey, surrounded
by the marbled metaphorical continents, blasting into the
Victorian fundament, on its way to sexual congress with its
mammarian / vulval partner the Royal Albert Hall, transmogri-
fying both into the copulatory Victoria and Albert Museum with
its thrusting towers and supple domes. Albertopolis, Victoria's
monument to her lover, is an area/ arena of death and desire, a
hallucinated topology of lack, absence, and death. The Albert
Memorial's phallocentric thrust embodies Victoria's symbolic
necrophilia in which Albert's dead body metamorphoses into a
giant gilded statue, a form of 'Venus statuaria,' love for or inter-

course with a statue as seen in the agalmatophilia of Krafft-Ebing's 'story of a young man (related by Lucianus and St. Clemens of Alexandria) who made use of a Venus of Praxiteles for the gratification of his lust; and the case of Clisyphus, who violated the statue of a goddess in the Temple of Samos, after having placed a piece of meat on a certain part. In modern times, the 'Journal L'evenement' of 4th March, 1877, relates the story of a gardener who fell in love with a statue of the Venus of Milo, and was discovered attempting coitus with it.'[98] An extreme form of Pygmalionism, Victoria's symbolic necrophilia, her building of memorials, concert halls, and museums for her dead lover, enacts a 'religious fetishism and phallus cult'[99] of Albert.

In the twentieth and twenty-first centuries, this symbolic necrophilia manifests itself in Salvador Dali and Luis Bunuel's *L'age d'or*, Jake and Dinos Chapman's *Death* (two bronzed inflatable dolls on a LI-LO in the 69 position), and the articulated/de-articulated dolls of Hans Bellmer, Katan Amano, Ryoichi Yoshida, Marina Bychkova and, more recently Sarah Lucas's *Black and White Bunny* and *Pauline Bunny*. The sex doll's inanimate concupiscence actualizes a symbolic necrophilia, its gradation of life-like appearance and touch made terminal and morbid by their thanatoid presence, their living absence. As dolls and robots become more human, the 'uncanny valley'[100] effect develops in which humans feel a revulsion to the robot/ doll, like the corpse, the doll/ robot is both nearly human and fully human and neither. Both the agalmatophile and the necrophile transgress this 'uncanny valley' and transform this revulsion into desire. In 2007, Erika LaBrie took part in a commitment ceremony with the Eiffel Tower and became Erica 'Aya' Eiffel (she has had previous 'commitments' to her archery bow and the Berlin Wall), in an objectum (object sexuality) variation of Victoria's symbolic necrophilia with the Albert Memorial. These acts strip 'sexuality of all functionality, whether biological or social; in an even more extreme fashion than "normal" sexuality, (they put) the body and the world of objects to uses that have nothing to do with any kind of "immanent" design or purpose.'[101] Achilles, Dimoetes, Herod, Greenlee, von Cosel, Bertrand and even Queen Victoria show that '[t]here is no form of human sexuality which does not marginalize need or substitute a fantasmatic object for the original and nutritive object.'[102] Maybe the necrophile, symbolic or not, discovers that 'the deepest chords of humanity are better struck through a dedicated artificiality than a simulation of humanness.'[103]

Sculptures of our dead ones, sarcophagi depicting the deceased, robots and dolls that present us with glimpses of our own mortality, are memento mori, objects projecting our future, prompts to remember that we too will die, that we will no longer be animate (animal). Does the sexual possession of a corpse disinhibit our own death drive? An incestuous and psychopathic tyrant, Periander of Corinth, (628–588 BCE)—one of the Seven Sages of Greece—accidentally killed his pregnant wife Melissa by throwing a footstool at her, he then defiled her corpse, burned alive his concubines, and sent his two sons away to become eunuchs. His obsession with his own death has all the makings of a Greek mystery or riddle. After his necrophiliac act, did his megalomania become so intense that his own death would be invisible, as if it had not or could not have happened, that there would be no memento mori to his own passing? To hide his place of burial, Periander 'instructed two young men to meet a third man at a predetermined place and kill and bury him. Then he arranged for four men to pursue the first two and kill and bury them. Then he arranged for a larger group of men to hunt down the four. Having made all the preparations, he went out to meet the two young men, for he, Periander, was the third man.'[104] Periander attempted to escape death by anonymity, by refusing the architecture of desire, As Diogenes Laertius wrote,

Grieve not because thou hast not gained thine end, But take

with gladness all the gods may send;
Be warned by Periander's fate, who died
Of grief that one desire should be denied.[105]

Moving into the present and the future, necrophilia has similarities to cybersex and online sex webcams. 'The attraction of cybersex is that, since we are dealing only with virtual partners, there is no harassment. This aspect of cyberspace—the idea of a space in which, because we are not directly interacting with real people, nobody is harassed and we are free to let go our most extreme fantasies—found its ultimate expression in a proposal which recently resurfaced in some circles in the US, a proposal to "rethink" the rights of necrophiles (those who desire to have sex with dead bodies). Why should they be deprived of it? The idea was formulated that, in the same way people sign permission for their organs to be use for medical purposes in the case of their sudden death, one should also allow them to sign permission for their bodies to be given to necrophiliacs.'[106] The British author/artist Stewart Home pre-empted this concept in his 'necrocards'. Similar to organ-donor cards, they carried the message: 'I support sexual liberation' and 'I want to help others experiment sexually after my death'. On the reverse of the card are tick boxes indicating the sexual preferences after death—'I request that after my death A. my body be used for any type of sexual activity or B. gay only. straight only. I do not wish to be dismembered or disfigured during necrophiliac sex. (tick as appropriate).'[107]

Both Žižek and Home, with varying degrees of humour, irony and icononoclasm, view the dead body as an object that becomes a commodity of desire, an erotic vessel, a sex doll; a receptacle not of a transgressive sexual act but a reference to the shifting paradigms and rhizomic networks of human morality and sexuality.[108]

4

Necronaut—Sergeant Bertrand

Sixteen years before Queen Victoria's beloved consort died, a French soldier, already eroticized by corpses and entrails had an idea. To satisfy his lust, rather than happening upon dead bodies, he would disinter them. It was 1845, France was moving toward the end of King Louis-Philippe's July Monarchy, the philosophies of Romanticism and Anarchism were provoking revolt, coups, and calls for democratic government. Across the English Channel, Sir John Franklin and 134 men set sail on HMS Erebus and HMS Terror in the tragic lost expedition to find the Northwest Passage; while across the Atlantic, Henry David Thoreau began his years of civil disobedience, living in a cabin near Walden Pond. Sergeant Bertrand, intent on his obsession, would begin his years of sexual disobedience by ripping out the guts of cadavers and masturbating over then.

Born in 1822 (or 1824), François Bertrand attended the theological seminary of Langres. As Bertrand described in his confessional interview with doctors after his capture, 'I began to masturbate at a very tender age without knowing what I was doing; I did not conceal myself from anyone. It was not until the age of eight or nine that I began to think of women, but this passion did not become really strong until the age of thirteen or fourteen.'[109] Facts about his early years are sketchy but Bertrand admits to one of the classic indicators of necrophilia and of serial killing, 'seeing that it was impossible for me to have human bodies, I sought out the dead bodies of animals, which I mutilated as I later mutilated those of women or men. I cut open their bellies, and after having torn out the entrails, I masturbated while looking at them.' These animals included horses, dogs and cats. Once he joined the army in 1842, his bestial necrophilia continued and he states that while at the army 'camp of Villette in 1844, I did not delay going to the Saint-Denis canal to take out animals that had been drowned, dogs, sheep.' As a young soldier, he was popular with comrades and attractive to women but his necrophiliac tendencies began to increase, 'In 1846 I was no longer satisfied with dead animals; I had to have living ones. At the camp of Villette as in all barracks, there were many dogs, which, belonging to no one, followed the soldiers indiscriminately. I resolved to take some of these dogs into the country and kill them ... I tore out their entrails.'

In Late February 1847, near Tours, in the village of Bléré, Sergeant Bertrand's company, part of the 74th Regiment, billeted near the East Cemetery. After a walk with a fellow soldier through the valleys and hills, Bertrand and his comrade in arms entered the cemetery. There, Bertrand saw the gravediggers' tools leaning against a tombstone, the grave next to it not fully filled in. His head started to throb violently, his heart racing. He ditched his friend in the village and quickly returned to the cemetery. Day labourers were working on vines next to the graveyard but this didn't perturb the sergeant. The day before, rain had made it impossible for the gravediggers to finish their job. He took up a shovel, unearthed the body, and struck it repeatedly with the shovel's sharp edge. One of the vine workers heard the sound of metal on flesh, the sergeant's excited grunts, and ran to the gates. The sergeant hid in the grave next to the half-dismembered corpse. When the labourer left to fetch the marshal, Bertrand filled in the grave and escaped by climbing over the cemetery wall. He hid in a copse, obscured by bushes, the undergrowth his mattress, delirious with lust and violence, two hours lost in oblivious revelry. Two nights later, in the pounding rain, he returned to the grave. The gravediggers had taken their tools, so the sergeant got down on his hands and knees and pulled up the sodden earth with his bloodied hands. He managed to disinter the lower part of the body and set about mutilating it with a knife, experiencing an orgasm as he cut into the flesh. Throughout March, April, and early May, he visited cemeteries in the surrounding districts in a state of erotic compulsion but either resisted or is deterred from consummating his lust. When unable to fully disinter a corpse, he would cut off a piece of the dead woman's clothing and use it to masturbate, or masturbate over it, beside the grave. Sergeant Bertrand goes beyond fantasy, beyond trophy taking, these remnant, onanistic objects, become Lacanian, '*objet a* ... something from which the subject, in order to constitute itself, has separated itself off as organ. This serves as a symbol of the lack, that is to say, of the phallus, not as such, but in so far as it is lacking. It must, therefore, be an object that is, firstly, separable and, secondly, that has some relation to the lack.'[110] Metonyms of masturbation, the pieces of clothing acting as replacements for the unattainable dead body, intimately connected with it but separate, that Bertrand re-organ-izes with the splash of his semen.

In May of 1847, back in Paris with his regiment, Bertrand's desires overcome his sensibilities. After walking around Père Lachaise Cemetery, scoping out access points, he decided to come back one evening. The cemetery, now popular after the remains of the tragic twelfth century lovers Abélard and Héloïse were transferred there in 1817, had walls surrounding it, but around 9pm, one June night, Bertrand climbed over and prowled the paths between the graves and tombs looking for an opportunity to exercise his dark ideas. He found a common grave that would allow him easy access and began to dig. Beneath the soil, he found the body of a 40-year-old woman. He disembowelled her and cut the entrails 'into a thousand pieces,' this satisfied him enough and he did not sexually abuse the corpse. Over the next two weeks, his obsession brought him to the cemetery most evenings, where he would dig up women and cut up their entrails but not sexually assault them—the mutilation enough for orgasm—he would masturbate while fondling the disembowelled organs or part of the corpse. He would then re-bury the body parts. One night, disturbed by guards who threatened to shoot him, he explained his way out of the predicament by saying he had drank too much and fallen asleep in the cemetery. This encounter with authorities scared him off for a time until his regiment left for Soissons in Picardy, but there the cemetery proved impossible to break into at night.

Interpreting Marx's analysis of the 1848 French Revolution and capitalism, Slavoj Žižek could be writing about Bertrand and his 'actual corrosive power which undermines all particular lifeworlds, cultures, and traditions, cutting across them, catching them in [his] vortex.'[111] In February 1848, just days before the end of the Orléans monarchy and the establishment of the Second Republic, Bertrand's personal vortex overwhelmed him with the urge to mutilate a body. Stationed in the northern town of Douai, on the 10th of March, after the bugle call at 8pm, Bertrand climbed the regiment's compound walls, swam across a wide and deep ditch filled with icy water. Once in the cemetery, he exhumed the body of a teenage girl, the first corpse with which he had full sexual intercourse. He fondled the 15-year-old's dead flesh, kissed her all over, hugged her passionately, caressed her breasts and buttocks. After 15 minutes of making love to the body, in the throes of an indescribable passion, he mutilated the girl and ripped out her viscera. He then re-interred the body and once again swam through the icy ditch and scaled the ruined walls of his barracks.

This escalation in Bertrand's necrophiliac desires results in an increase in his exhumation of and intercourse with corpses. In Lille, from late March over a period of a month, he disinterred four women and has sexual intercourse with their bodies before eviscerating and mutilating them. On a few occasions, the hardness of the ground made it impossible for him to dig up corpses, this happened in Doullens in early July, the summer sun baking the earth until Bertrand tore his nails trying to dig his way down. At the end of July, back in Paris, in the middle of the 1848 revolution, the guards at the regiment's camp at Ivry-sur-Seine had it under lockdown but Bertrand's desires meant he had to escape. Each night, he found a way out and made his way to Montparnasse cemetery. On the 25th of July, he disinterred and had sex with the badly decomposed body of a twelve-year-old girl, after disembowelling her and mutilating her genitals, he masturbated over the corpse. One night, he dug up two bodies and carried them to a tomb where he would not be disturbed by the armed guards, he had sex with the body of a 60-year-old woman but left the corpse of the three-year-old girl untouched.

Were these acts sexual reproductions of the violence in French and European culture at the time? Marx wrote of the June days of the 1848 revolution that 'The tricolour republic now bears only one colour, the colour of the defeated, the colour of blood. It has become the red republic.' That 'the Paris of the proletariat burned, bled and moaned in its death agony.' And that 'The June revolution is the ugly revolution, the repulsive revolution, because realities have taken the place of words, because the republic has uncovered the head of the monster itself by striking aside the protective, concealing crown.'[112] Did the fomentation of social revolt lead to a fermentation of sexual rebellion, of revolting erotic desires?

In a cemetery closer to the camp in Ivry, over a period of a month, Bertrand copulated with the bodies of a girl aged seven and a woman in her late thirties, mutilating the young girl but not disembowelling either body. Finding Montparnasse too difficult to break into, Bertrand visited hospital and suicide graveyards. Unable to find the bodies of women, he took out his anger by digging up male corpses and, repulsed by them, slashing them with his sabre. In the space of four months, he exhumed fifteen bodies, only two of which were women. His anger and sexual frustration escalating, he had sex with the women, eviscerated them, split their mouths to a Joker smile, cut their bodies to ribbons, pulled at their limbs, twisting the bodies into grotesque shapes in an attempt to 'destroy' them, he would then masturbate.

Toward the end of this period of escalation, at 10pm on the 6th of November, guards fired a shot at Bertrand as he climbed over the wall into the cemetery, the bullets missed and Bertrand waited two hours on cold and wet stone steps before re-entering. Once in, he dug up the recently buried body of a woman in her mid-twenties, a well-preserved victim of drowning. Again, he eviscerated her, mutilated her genitals, and made a deep cut through to the bone in her left thigh—with this corpse, he achieved a greater orgasm than with previous ones and hoped that the intensity would satiate his violent and dark desires.

His cravings were becoming uncontrollable and he stated that '[I]n all my violations of sepulchres, in no case was the act premeditated; when the attack got possession of me, whether at noon or at midnight, I had to go; it was impossible to postpone it.' and in December guards shot at him, the bullet tearing through his greatcoat. He fled into the storm-ridden night but re-crossed the muddy fields to the Ivry cemetery where he attempted without success to exhume a corpse. In January 1849 in Montparnasse, another shot rang out as he escaped the traps the guards set for him and the dogs prowling the pathways.

Leaving the Luxembourg Gardens on Thursday the 15th of March, Bertrand tried to break into Montparnasse by climbing the walls but a booby-trapped gun shot him. Bloodied from wounds along his right side, Bertrand arrived at the Val-de-Grâce military hospital at 11:30pm. The story of his wounds soon started circulating and became the gossip of soldiers. A Montparnasse cemetery gravedigger heard about the story and informed authorities, and police visited the hospital to arrest Bertrand. One of his surgeons, Dr Marchal de Calvi, took down Bertrand's confession and the prosecution used the notes at Bertrand's trial—as necrophilia did not exist as a crime, the court found Sergeant François Bertrand guilty of vampirism.

If the escalation in Bertrand's perversions culminated in his capture, what were the origins of that perversion and what tipped dark fantasy into darker reality? As Foucault states, in the nineteenth century, 'sex gradually became an object of great suspicion; the general and disquieting meaning that pervades our existence, in spite of ourselves; the point of weakness where evil portents reach through to us; the fragment of darkness that we each carry with us: a general signification, a universal secret, an omnipresent cause, a fear that never ends.'[113]

In the opening decade of the twenty-first century, Philippines police dubbed a successor to Sergeant Bertrand the 'Tomb Raider.' At first, local residents thought a gang of necrophiles was responsible for the disinterred female corpses spread-eagled on tombs. In the small Barangay of Mercedes, over a period of six months between October 2009 and May 2010, local people found five bodies laid out on their own graves, all had been sexually abused. The victims ranged in age from an elderly woman to a 13-day-old girl. Other victims included a 17-year-old student and a female teacher found hanging naked from a post. After a few false leads, police arrested 19-year-old Randy Uro Galvez for breaking into tombs at two cemeteries in Mercedes. Nonito Toribio Sr., the acting caretaker of the Mercedes New Cemetery caught Galvez with a slab of wood and a stick with which he hammered open the tombs and desecrated them. In June 2010, the Philippines Government proposed Senate Bill 1038 making necrophilia illegal. Previously, sexual intercourse with a female corpse was 'beyond the pale'[114] of the criminal justice system and the bill hoped to 'plug this distinct lacuna in the law by penalizing necrophiles or those who morbidly derive sexual gratification by copulating with a corpse. That such forcible imposition of manhood is directed against a lifeless female does not make the grisly act and less detestable and heinous. In fact, this vicious bestiality is notoriously offensive and revolting to the feelings of the living even as it grossly desecrates the dead.' The Senate passed the bill and imposed a death penalty for the crime. While Galvez awaited trial for the alleged assaults, in the Philippines town of San Jose, a cemetery worker discovered the exhumed naked body of 15-year-old high-school student Jay Molina who had been killed in a motor accident a week earlier; a medical examiner found evidence of rape.

Both Bertrand and the Tomb Raider suffer from 'Ophelia's Grave' syndrome, acting out a desire to 'Hold off the earth awhile / Till I have caught her once more in mine arms,'[115] the earth a return to the womb and a drive toward their own death. Like Laertes who 'leaps into the grave and embraces the object whose loss is the cause of his desire, an object that has attained an existence that is all the more absolute because it no longer corresponds to anything in reality. The one unbearable dimension of possible human existence is not the experience of one's own death, which no one has, but the experience of the death of another,'[116] both Bertrand and the Tomb Raider, like Marx's Paris of June 1848, impose new realities, new sexual landscapes. For both men, the desecration of the grave, the act of exhumation, the laying out of the corpse, ritualized the act of necrophilia; Bertrand added mutilation to his sexual rites, whereas the Tomb Raider preferred humiliation—he left the body of the teacher hanging from a post suspended by her stockings with her underwear removed and placed over her head. Where Bertrand mostly placed the bodies back in the grave, the Tomb Raider left them on display—Bertrand a humble Laertes to the Tomb Raider's histrionic Hamlet—each a double of the other, separated by a quarter of a millennium, they come together in an orgy of death, lust, and desecration. These examples of necrophilia stem from the stuff of myth, of vampires and werewolves, digging corpses from graves with their bare hands, smashing sepulchres with hammers, levering lids from coffins, grave robbers and bodysnatchers, an unholy amalgamation of Dracula, Ed Gein, and Burke and Hare, yet both men are classified as 'classic' or 'regular' necrophiles, what Wulffen termed 'necrostuprum'[117] or grave robbers, necrophiles who use already dead bodies as sex object. Although they mutilate, they do not murder to obtain a body.

Initially, sexologists considered necrophilia a form of sadism, yet Bertrand could inflict no pain on the bodies. Indeed, the amount of pain he went through getting to the corpse or escaping the guards and dogs, made the savage lust his own personal form of necrophilia—necromasochism. Often necrophiles become so through rejection by the opposite sex, but Bertrand had intercourse with living women in the different towns he visited with the army; apparently a good lover, women vowed to marry him.[118] Despite this, every two weeks or so, Bertrand would suffer from intense headaches and become obsessed with a desire for violence and violation, despite the weather, icy waters, frozen or baked earth, guns and booby traps. The necromasochism flipped into necrosadism as a means to enhance the sexual thrill, mutilation as foreplay. Epaulard quotes from Marchal de Calvi's interview where Bertrand confessed, 'I have always loved women madly; I have permitted no one to insult them in my presence. I have everywhere had young and charming women as mistresses, whom I have completely satisfied and who have yielded very willingly to me. As proof of this, some, although of rich and distinguished family, have wanted to follow me. I have never touched a married woman. Indecent talk has always offended me. I always tried to bring the conversation to another channel, when such a theme was broached in my presence. I was brought up strictly religious; I have always cared for religion and defended it, but without fanaticism.'

In the late nineteenth century, the Socialist criminologist Enrico Ferri stated 'Again, there are the necrophiles, like Sergeant Bertrand, Verzeni, Menesclou, and very probably the undetected "Jack the Ripper" of London, who are tainted with a form of sexual psychopathy. Yet again there are such as are tainted with hereditary madness, and especially the epileptics and epileptoids, who may also be assigned to the class of born criminals, according to the plausible hypothesis of Lombroso as to the fundamental identity of congenital criminality, moral madness, and epilepsy. I have always found in my own experience that outrageous murders, not to be explained according to the ordinary psychology of criminals, are accompanied by psychical epilepsy, or larvea.'[119]

5

NecroGermania

Sexual psychopaths and sadistic killers do not always become necrophiles, nor do they all mutilate corpses, but some are only able to experience orgasm at the point of another's death, during the act of murder or attempted murder—the death of their victims at the point of the killer's orgasm make them necrophiles by projection. If the authorities mythologized Sergeant Bertrand as the Vampire of Montparnasse, 80 years later and 250 miles from Paris, the German police, in order to comprehend the perpetrator of a spate of vicious sex murders, searched for a man the newspapers were calling the Vampire of Düsseldorf.[120]

Born on 26 May 1883 in the Mülheim district of Köln (Cologne), Peter Kürten spent his poverty-stricken childhood in a one-roomed apartment with thirteen younger brothers and sisters. His alcoholic and sexiopathic father subjected the family to violence and his mother and sisters to rape and attempted rape. The children witnessed their father's violent sexual assaults and incestuous intercourse with his thirteen-year-old daughter and these events—plus his father's incarceration for attempted incest—fuelled Peter's sadistic childhood fantasies. As in many cases of serial murder and necrophilia, Peter began his career of depravity by inflicting violence and sex on animals. These were all mechanisms of defamiliarization.

A dogcatcher lived in the Kürten house, and the man taught Peter how to torture dogs and showed him how to sexually excite them. In this, Peter transferred his father's sexual violence on to strays that roamed the fortified German city, enlisting the brutal dogcatcher as his father figure. At the age of ten, while boating on the Rhine, Peter drowned another boy and attempted to drown yet another who came to his friend's aid. As he moved into puberty, the sexual manipulation and torture of dogs and the thrill he felt whilst drowning the boy developed into oricide and hiricide as he repeatedly stabbed sheep and goats while having intercourse with them.

By the turn of the century, Peter had been arrested and imprisoned for theft on a number of occasions and would spend 24 years of his life in prison mostly in Düsseldorf. In 1899, he met a prostitute who allowed him to explore his sadistic side, and he now had a human outlet for his sexual fantasies, her masochism fuelling his violent lust.

Published in the same year that Peter met his masochistic partner, Octave Mirbeau's *Le Jardin des supplices* (*The Torture Garden*) hints at the reasoning Kürten used to justify the escalation of his violent lust to sexual murder. 'You're obliged to pretend respect for people and institutions you think absurd. You live attached in a cowardly fashion to moral and social conventions you despise, condemn, and know lack all foundation. It is that permanent contradiction between your ideas and desires and all the dead formalities and vain pretences of your civilization which makes you sad, troubled and unbalanced. In that intolerable conflict you lose all joy of life and all feeling of personality, because at every moment they suppress and restrain and check the free play of your powers. That's the poisoned and mortal wound of the civilized world.'[121]

The German industrial revolution had swelled the population of Düsseldorf and increased the alienation of its citizens, after defeat in World War I and the occupation by French and British armies, itinerant workers, beggars, and thieves roamed the cities—perfect for any would-be serial killer. While in prison, Peter had elaborated and perfected his unreal universe, his anti-human philosophy. In the introduction to *The Torture Garden*, Tom McCarthy writes, 'For the idealist Hegel, the material world is there to be abstracted by the philosopher or artist into thought, into pure, sublimated concept. Hegel's most famous commentator, Kojève, describes this sublimating process as a form of murder. It is hard not to hear an echo (or, again, pre-echo) of this description in the conversations of Mirbeau's philosophers, poets and moralists who talk of "backs on the street which cry out for the knife" or his explorer who envisages a bullet "which will annihilate what it hits, leaving nothing."'

Kürten's perversity meant annihilation of the other, the event of murder forming a complete absence of person, a negative humanity; he would transgress prison law in order to be placed in solitary confinement, and his detachment from others meant he could fantasize without the need to socialize. Kürten killed men, women, children, and animals—to Peter, every back cried out for a knife, everything existed to be annihilated, to be completely destroyed. Kürten had no understanding of his *Gattungswesen* (social-being), his life embodied Marx's theories of alienation, 'The class of the proletariat feels annihilated, this means that they cease to exist in estrangement; it sees in it its own powerlessness and the reality of an inhuman existence. It is, to use an expression of Hegel, in its abasement the indignation at that abasement, an indignation to which it is necessarily driven by the contradiction between its human nature and its condition of life, which is the outright, resolute and comprehensive negation of that nature. Within this antithesis the private property-owner is therefore the conservative side, the proletarian the destructive side. From the former arises the action of preserving the antithesis, from the latter the action of annihilating it.'[122]

It's interesting to note that Marx and Engels collaborated on this essay in Paris in 1844, a few months before Bertrand's necrophiliac atrocities escalated.

On the 25th of May 1913, Kürten burgles an inn on the Wolfstrasse in Köln, he searches the ground floor and, finding nothing worth stealing, walks up the stairs to where the family sleeps. He looks in the rooms and in one finds a 10-year-old girl—Christine Klein—sleeping under a feather blanket. He grabs the girl by the throat and strangles her, excited by the girl's pathetic struggling. The girl passes out and Kürten strips her and pushes his fingers into her vagina. He then takes out a pocketknife, holds the girl's head back and slashes her throat. He listens to the blood pump out and drip onto the carpet, some of it splashes across his hand in rhythmic arcs. As she dies, he bites her tongue, punctures her throat twice with the knife. It takes three minutes for her to die and he leaves her body on the bed and returns to Düsseldorf. The next day, he goes back to the scene of the crime and drinks beer in a café with a view of the inn, listening to people talk about the crime, the horror of others excited him and the murder of the girl stimulated his pathological sadism.

In the same year, the literary journal Arcadia published Franz Kafka's 'Das Urteil' ('The Judgement') in which a son grapples with the legacy and disappointment of his bullying and disapproving father. The old man eventually condemns his son to death by water, proclaiming, 'So now you know what else there was besides yourself; up till now all you knew was you! You were an innocent child, really, but it would be truer to say you were a veritable fiend!'[123] The son runs through the city streets to the river, leaps over parapets and clings to the rails until he weakens and drops, and 'At that moment, a quite unending flow of traffic streamed over the bridge.'[124] Kafka admitted to Max Brod that the last line meant a 'violent ejaculation.'[125]

Kürten's inaugural murder, the primal escalation of his death lust either re-enacts the sexual onslaughts his father perpetrated on his mother and sisters, or protects the young girl from further harm. Police found a 9cm-long cut on the girl's throat but no signs of phallic rape. After digitally penetrating her, Kürten had incised a new unpenetrated vagina on the girl's neck, the blood coursing over the bridge of his hand, as a 'violent ejaculation,' the blood as metaphor for his own compulsive masturbation, the site

and sight, the feel of his own ejaculative emission while fantasizing about the event now actualized.

In 1920, with Kürten in prison for arson and theft, Düsseldorf
was at the forefront of the German General Strike as part of the
Ruhr uprising, a left-wing and communist workers' revolt. Over
300,000 miners and other workers took control of Düsseldorf.
The Freikorps—a paramilitary militia—murdered 45 striking
miners on the 15th of April 1920. Adolf Hitler, in a speech on 13
July 1934, included the Friekorps in his list of 'pathological
enemies of the state,' revealing that he had read a diary from
1918 that provided: '…an insight into the mentality of people
who, without realizing it, have found in nihilism their ultimate
creed. Incapable of any real cooperation, determined to take a
stand against any kind of order filled by hatred of every
authority as they are their uneasiness and their restless this can
be quelled only by their permanent mental and conspiratorial
preoccupation with the disintegration whatever exists at the
given time.'[126]

In 1921, a year after the release of expressionist film *The
Cabinet of Dr Caligari* in which the somnambulist Cesare abducts
and murders young women, Kürten left prison, married and
worked in a factory where he became a political activist involved
in trade unionism. In the midst of the Weimar Republic's political
violence, his own pathological revolution fell into remission but,
in 1925, he was imprisoned again for theft and arson. The
fourteen years of the Weimar Republic—'a tumultuous inter-
regnum between disasters'[127]—instituted state violence, authori-
tarianism, and propaganda. A civilization of repression,
aggression dislocation—subjects of special interest to Theodor
Adorno, Herbert Marcuse, and Erich Fromm, all members of the
contemporaneous Frankfurt School. Fromm would go on to
write extensively about necrophilia and the necrophilious
character.

During his spell in prison, Kürten's sadistic fantasies intensified, on the 9th of February 1929, they spilled over into lust murder; this time, Rosa Ohliger—an eight-year-old-girl—would be his victim. He had perfected the attack with a series of assaults on women in the days leading up to the murder, stabbing one woman twenty four times. Düsseldorf police discovered her body half hidden under a hedge, they found thirteen stab wounds on her body and evidence that the killer had tried to burn it. Kürten had again returned to the scene and orgasmed as he had when setting fire to the young girl's body. During the autopsy, doctors found knife wounds and semen traces in and around the girl's vagina and ejaculate on her underwear.

Kürten killed the girl ten days after the first publication of Erich Maria Remarque's *Im Westen nichts Neues* (*All Quiet on the Western Front*) portraying the trauma experienced by soldiers in the First World War, the alienation they felt in trying to adapt to society, and the deprivation they faced in a time of economic depression. In prison throughout most of the war, Kürten must have felt an existential if not ethical kinship with these soldiers, traumatized as he was by his father, a criminal alienated within society, thieving to make a living.

If he did feel empathy towards the soldiers, he felt nothing for the ordinary citizens (and animals) of Düsseldorf. On the 14th of February—as Al Capone's men were using machine guns and shotguns to mow down members of Bugs Moran's gang in the St Valentine's Day massacre in Chicago—in Flingern, Kürten stabbed a 45-year-old mechanic 20 times and watched him bleed to death. He returned later and spoke to police investigating the crime.

On 21 August, Kürten heard the 'backs on the street which cry out for the knife,' bidding passers-by in Lierenfeld a 'Good evening,' and then stabbing them in their backs and in their ribs. At 10:30pm, two days later, in Flehe, Gertrude Hamacher (aged five) and Louise Lenzen (14) were walking home together after the annual fair. Kürten emerged from the trees, gave money to

Louise and asked her to buy him cigarettes. When Louise left, Kürten strangled Gertrude and cut her throat with a knife. When Louise returned, Kürten pulled her into the bushes, strangled and then decapitated her. The next day, after propositioning a servant girl—Gertrude Schulte—for sex, he stabbed her and fled. The girl survived and gave the police a description of the 'pleasant-looking' man.

In September 1929, Kürten raped and beat to death Ida Reuter; on the 12th of October, he did the same to Elizabeth Dorrier; and on the 25th of October, he attacked Frau Meurer and Frau Wanders with a hammer. On the 9th of November, a local newspaper received a letter with a map showing the whereabouts of a dead child—police found the strangled and mutilated body of five-year-old Gertrude Albermann outside an abandoned factory. To avoid capture—or to shift the dynamics of his orgasms—over the next six months, Kürten changed his modus operandi, baffling police and terrorizing the city.

On the 14th of May 1930, Maria Budlick journeyed from Köln to Düsseldorf. At Düsseldorf station, a man approached her and said he would show her a cheap women's hostel where she could stay while looking for work. She followed the man but, recalling what she had read in the newspapers about the Düsseldorf vampire, she became suspicious. She quarrelled with the man until a passer-by intervened and chased the man off. Maria Budlick's saviour proved to be Peter Kürten and he took her to his room on Mettmanner Strasse. The young woman refused to have sex with Kürten and begged to leave, so Kürten took her to Worringerplatz by tram and from there through the Hellweg (salt road or way of the dead) to the Grafenberger Woods. Kürten had used the wood before, attempting to murder a girl while raping her, he had left the girl there but her body was never discovered. This time, under the cover of the trees, Kürten grabbed Maria's throat and repeated his demands for intercourse. Whatever her reply, he attempted to rape her and then showed her the way to the tram station. Fraulein Budlick then wrote to a friend—Frau Bruckner—but the post delivered the letter by mistake to a Frau Brugmann who, after reading the contents, took it to the police. Kürten did not think the young woman would remember the direction to his apartment at 71 Mettmanner Strasse, but a week later, after she had been questioned by the police, Chief Inspector Gennat escorted her to the address. While they were there, Kürten returned home, passed them on the stairs, and went into his room, changed and left the building under the observation of two plainclothes police officers. He returned to his wife, admitted the crime, and two days later told her about the other attacks and confessed that he was the Düsseldorf Vampire. He told her that if he had to go to prison for the rest of his life, she should inform on him to the police and collect the reward money. On the 24th of May, Frau Kürten contacted the police and told them of her husband's confessions. If they came to St Rochus church at 3pm, her husband would be there to meet her. Armed police ambushed Kürten but the vampire went with them peacefully, saying, 'There is no need to be afraid.'

While awaiting trial, the psychologist Professor Karl Berg interviewed Kürten who openly confessed his crimes and perversions. Whereas Bertrand had little recollection of his deeds, blinded by a quasi-epileptic light, Kürten had almost total recall. For him, remembering the details of his crimes was almost as stimulating as dismembering the corpses. However, he struggled to recall other facts about his life and blamed society for what he had become. A stenographer recorded the sadistic events as Kürten admitted nearly 80 sexual and violent crimes against men, women, and children, smiling as he shocked the attendant police officers with the precision of his recall.

On the 13th of April 1931, standing in a specially constructed cage, Kürten answered charges of nine murders and seven attempted murders. The prosecution displayed the clothes, skulls, and mutilated body parts of the Vampire's victims, along with the tools of his crime—a hammer, a spade, rope, scissor, and various knives. Contemporary photos of Kürten show a respectable, well-dressed and well-built middle-aged man. Despite his confession, he denied the charges and pleaded not guilty. After two months of examining and cross-examining, the prosecution eventually pressured Kürten into changing his plea to guilty and the court heard his original confession, despite Dr Berg's promise to him that it would be kept between them. The medical profession attested to Kürten's sanity. Kürten held to his belief that the motive for his homicidal sexual attacks had been to take revenge on a society that had subjected him to the brutalities of the prison system. Kürten admitted to the judge that he had no conscience, no empathy or sympathy for his victims, just as his torturers (prison guards and father) had no guilt for what they had done. He did not believe his actions were evil; they were revenge for the injustices inflicted upon him, what had happened to him had made him a pitiless non-human. He blamed god, his father, the courts, prison, and Germany for his sadistic nature, which included fantasies of mass murder, admitting, 'I derived the sort of pleasure from these visions that other people would get from thinking about a naked woman.' Kürten's veracity of narrative matched the voracity of his crimes, and the prosecution sat back and allowed him to damn himself while his defence counsel, Dr Wehner, attempted to prove his client's insanity. Faced with the confession, evidence, and Kürten's obvious selfish enjoyment in the retelling, the jury took just 90 minutes to find him guilty of all charges. Dr Rose, the judge, sentenced him to death on each of the nine murder counts. Kürten accepted the penalty, even though he fastidiously questioned the evidence of the witnesses when it clashed with his apparent superior memory of events, and he thought the medical and psychological evidence inaccurate.

Unknowingly, Kürten had reinforced and foreseen Freud's

theories in *Totem and Taboo* (1913) and *Civilization and Its Discontents* (1930)—the horror of incest, sexuality and violence, society's laws against the individual's narcissistic and erotic desires. Freud, like Marx before him, saw man as increasingly alienated. Kürten embodied Freud's theories and enacted civilization's ultimate discontents. 'The bit of truth behind all this—one so eagerly denied—is that men are not gentle, friendly creatures wishing for love, who simply defend themselves if they are attacked, but that a powerful measure of desire for aggression has to be reckoned as part of their instinctual endowment. The result is that their neighbour is to them not only a possible helper or sexual object, but also a temptation to them to gratify their aggressiveness on him, to exploit his capacity for work without recompense, to use him sexually without his consent, to seize his possessions, to humiliate him, to cause him pain, to torture and kill him. *Homo homini lupus.*'[128] The Werewolf of Düsseldorf.

Engineers built a specially designed guillotine in the yard of Köln's Klingelputz prison. On the final walk to his death, Kürten asked his doctor, 'After my head has been chopped off, will I still be able to hear, at least for a moment, the sound of my own blood gushing from the stump of my neck? That would be the pleasure to end all pleasures.'

Although never confessing to necrophilia, Kürten's crimes indicate that he almost certainly used death as a sexual stimulant and as a means to orgasm. Whereas Bertrand felt disgust at the sight of the body of a dead male, Kürten killed regardless of age, sex, and even species. Both men lived in the solipsistic world of the sexual psychopath in which they were the prime being—nothing and nobody mattered when it came to satiating their lust. Both were sadistic narcissists who could not establish relationships with other human beings. Where Bertrand had headaches until he had satisfied his obsession, Kürten felt a building tension until the conclusion of the violent sex event. Both men enjoyed the danger of their crimes, Bertrand evading guards, fording icy ditches, while Kürten returned to the scene of his crimes or stayed to watch the bodies burn and listen to the screams. Could both men have been abused as children? Could they have fostered their lust for death as revenge fantasies? Both men lived outward lives of respectability, so what germinated their perversions?

Is there a socio-historic cause? Carl Grossmann (1863–1922), a sadistic sexual predator and child molester, killed and cannibalized up to 50 women, the court found the Bluebeard of the Silesian Railways guilty of 14 sex-killings and sentenced him to death. Grossmann hanged himself before the execution. Karl Denke (1870–1924) the Münsterberg Mass Murderer, a quiet recluse, respected in his neighbourhood, murdered and cannibalized 30 people over a 20-year period. When police searched his house they found curing jars containing human flesh, amputated fingers, teeth, and items made from human skin. Denke also hanged himself before trial. Friedrich 'Fritz' Haarmann (1879 –1925) sexually murdered 27 young men and boys between 1918 and 1924. He considered his execution for 24 of these killings as the ultimate means of orgasm. Haarmann killed his victims by ripping out their throats with his teeth and strangling them in the act of sodomy, he threw what remained of the dismembered corpses in the Leine river—the media called him the Vampire of Hanover and the Butcher of Hanover.

Robert Musil (November 6, 1880–April 15, 1942), Peter Kürten (26 May 1883–2 July 1931), Franz Kafka (3 July 1883–3 June 1924), Adolf Hitler (20 April 1889–30 April 1945), Ludwig Wittgenstein (26 April 1889–29 April 1951), Martin Heidegger (September 26, 1889–May 26, 1976), John Heartfield (19 June 1891–26 April 1968), Walter Benjamin (1892–1940), George Grosz (26 July 1893–6 July 1959), The social and economic privations after the First World War, the German Revolution of 1918, and the Weimar Republic (1918–33) caused an explosion of avant-garde art, literature, and film, and a commensurate increase in sex killing and cannibalism. Of the four lust murderers who stalked Germany in the 1920s, four practised necrosadism, three necrophagy, and suspicion must fall on all of them for being necrophiles.

The exploits of these murderers found their way into literature in the character of the psychopathic Moosbrugger in Musil's *The Man Without Qualities* (1930–42), Vladimir Nabokov's *Despair* (1934)—written while Nabokov was living in Berlin, D.M. Thomas's *The White Hotel* (1981), and Patrick Süskind's *Perfume* (1985). A late German Expressionist film—and forerunner of film noir—premiered on 11 May 1931 while Peter Kürten awaited execution. Set in Berlin, the crimes of the paedophiliac sex killer Hans Beckert, played by Peter Lorre, are similar to those of Grossmann, Denke, Haarmann, and Kürten, the film portraying a city (Berlin) terrorized—as Paris, Hanover, and Düsseldorf had been—by a necrosadist.

Throughout the film, the sex-killer whistles the refrain 'In the Hall of the Mountain King' from Edvard Grieg's Peer Gynt, the lyrics of which could have been sung in disharmony by the barbarous quartet of Kürten, Grossmann, Haarmann and Denke:

May I hack him on the fingers?
May I tug him by the hair?
Hu, hey, let me bite him in the haunches!
Shall he be boiled into broth and bree to me
Shall he roast on a spit or be browned in a stewpan?

Cut to: Patch of scrub bordered by trees (Berlin's Grunewald forest standing in for Düsseldorf's Grafenberger Woods), a small ball rolls out of the undergrowth and rocks to a stop. Cut to: Child's balloon, anthropomorphic, all torso and head, spastically dancing against overhead electric wires—a young girl is murdered, maybe raped, and a city searches for her killer—Fritz Lang's *M*.

29 years later, a basement (abasement), a young woman

touches the shoulder of an old lady and the chair she is sitting on swivels around in a rocking chair to reveal a mummified (mummyfied) corpse, skin shrivelled to the skull, teeth revealed to their roots, a dark void where once were eyes. The young woman screams, turns to run, a lightbulb swings giving the room a German-Expressionist chiaroscuro. As she screams, another old woman lunges through the door wielding a knife, a man follows and grapples with her, in the struggle, the woman's wig falls off revealing a young man dressed as his dead mother — Alfred Hitchcock's *Psycho*.

Slavoj Žižek[129] argues that the mother's house in Psycho reproduces the three levels of human subjectivity. The ground floor is ego where Norman acts as a normal son. The first floor is the super-ego in the figure of the dead mother. Down in the cellar is the id — the reservoir of illicit drives. When Norman carries his mother's mummified corpse down to the basement, it's as though he were transferring the super-ego to the id. Žižek — through Freud[130] — sees the super-ego as an obscene agency perpetually bombarding the self with impossible orders, unapplicable ethics, unrealizable morals, that make us feel guilty for not achieving (or heeding) its dictums. Both Bertrand and Kürten had unsuccessful relationships with their fathers, they had no identification with the parental agency. If the installation of the super-ego can be described as a successful instance of identification with the parental agency, these men were failures, their super-egotistical striving for perfection retarded at an early age, they did not develop a conscience to control their fantasies, drives, and actions. Without a regulatory super-ego they did not feel guilt. Both Bertrand and Kürten simulated a super-ego in their dress, manner, and occupations, yet neither had any conception of social acceptability. If the super-ego is the regulatory control of the father internalized, then Bertrand and Kürten were without the father, without conscience, without morality and taboo, both men living in a perpetual Oedipal complex stage, the fear of castration transferred to the other—the other as victim. It could be argued that revolutionary France and Weimar Republic Germany had shifting and inchoate super-egos, the cultural and personal super-ego—which should be inter-locked—fractured and formed these men in worlds of relative morality and transitional ethics because a cultural super-ego 'does not trouble itself enough about the facts of the mental constitution of human beings.'[131]

If the cellar, basement, tomb represents the id—the arena of abasement—then that is where the necrophile resides, in the realm of the 'pleasure principle,' the unconscious becomes the freedom from tension (Bertrand's blackouts and Kürten's need to release built-up pressure). This is Freud's 'chaos, a cauldron full of seething excitations' in which 'contrary impulses exist side by side, without cancelling each other out.' Neither Bertrand or Kürten can be considered evil because they do not understand the concept, their pleasure instinct existing alongside their death drive, the bodies they kill, they have sex with, they mutilate are an attempt to 'lead organic life back into the inanimate state.'[132] Bertrand and Kürten's sexual and violent psychopathic events were 'instinct(s) of destruction directed against the external world and other organisms.'[133] Or, in Bertrand's case, destruction directed against the internal organs. He did this to destroy the human—Bertrand the id-machine, the dead but made alive, made dead bodies, fuel to his libido, his virtual reality powered by his libido that is always/ already firing his fantasies. The fantasy realized is sustained by extreme violence. Discussing the implied necrophilia in Hitchcock's Vertigo, Žižek claims the fantasy is realized as 'a process of mortification, which also is the mortifi-cation of woman's desire. It is as if in order to have her, to desire her, to have sexual intercourse with her, with the woman, Scottie has to mortify her, to change her into a dead woman. It's as if, again, for the male libidinal economy, to paraphrase a well-known old saying, the only good woman is a dead woman.'

6

NecroCinema—Prohibition, Inhibition, Exhibition

From the outside, the building resembles a classic American house, all apple pie and brilliant smiles: white clapboard, porch swing, all framed by a blue sky embroidered with puffy white clouds. A young woman—Pam—dressed in halter-neck, red shorts, walks into the house looking for her boyfriend Kirk. In the dark hallway, she hears a noise—something like large blades slicing against one another. In the background, the incessant hum of a generator. She pushes open heavy curtains, trips, and falls on to the floor. Beneath her fingers, thousands of feathers, and within the feathery undergrowth, hundreds of bones. A fat chicken in a too-small cage clucks and pecks at the bars. Pam looks around the room, the floor is littered with femurs, mandibles, the tarsals, metatarsals, and phalanges of a human foot. She looks up and sees that the foot connects to a tibia, but then the skeleton becomes deterritorialized. The phalanages, metacarpals, and carpals of a human hand lead to an ulna and radius, which in turn lead to a non-human connective bone attached by leather ties to a human skull flanked by a pair of cow scapula. (So far, so Hans Bellmer.) As the camera pans out, the monstrous assemblage resembles a shrine. As Pam looks around the room in terror, she sees various skeletal remains, human and animal, tied together with string or mounted on the walls—a human skull with a bull's horn penetrating its jaws, a turtle carapace, a tiny thoracic cage. On her hands and knees, she vomits in the ossuary/ fetish/ altar/ shrine. Choking and panicking, shouting for her boyfriend Kirk, Pam stumbles out of the room into the corridor. A metal door slides open—the door should not be there, it has no right to be in the dream house, it

73

has been transported there from the slaughterhouse, from the nightmare, from Père Lachais, from Düsseldorf. A man wearing a butcher's apron catches her and, laughing, carries her screaming back into the house and into the room beyond the sliding metal door. Once inside, he lifts her—still screaming—on to a large butcher's hook, a human body on the slab in front of her. The man crosses to a sink area and revs up a chain saw. It is then that we get a proper glimpse of his mask—it is made from segments of human faces, the skin stitched together with black leather thread. Later. Sally, having witnessed her wheelchair-bound brother sliced open by the chainsaw-wielding masked man, flees into the dream house, runs upstairs to the attic. Applying Žižek's psychological house rules, Sally flees into what she hopes is the super-ego, the arena of control, the realm of conscience, the antithesis to the id-wielding masked man. But there—in a similar way to the discovery of the mummified corpse in Psycho—she discovers the desiccated corpse of an old woman, and the near-to-death body of an old man—who turns out to be the grandfather—the super-ego near extinction. Later. Sally's fingers are bled and the blood fed to the corpse-like grandfather (resembling an animatronic William S. Burroughs), who sucks her fingers, a perverse oral sexuality, and gains strength as he does so.

Norman Bates and Leatherface are monstrous realizations of our own repressive desires and, concurrently, manifestations of oppressive economic transferences of otherness. In The Texas Chain Saw Massacre,[134] the two couples are split up (literally and viscerally in one case), their sexual and potentially familial normality sundered. Leatherface's 'family,' ostensibly driven to cannibalism by the mechanical automation of the slaughter-house—their 'otherness' played out in their unemployment and their necrophagy—threaten the status quo, threaten the perception of the human in its emancipated desires. Both monsters—Norman and Leatherface (and Bertrand by association)—represent their particular culture in crisis. All attempt to annihilate women from their twisted all-male families, or Bertrand's military substitute. Bates, Leatherface, and Bertrand deny the human, deny the possibilities of normality, of capitalist society, and of reproduction.

For Bates, Leatherface, and Bertrand, the society (and family) they resided in was under threat from outside sources—Communism, America's defeat in Vietnam, revolutionary France. They react to this rupture by living transgressive versions of the family (society's minimalist mirror) as an animadversion of the existing culture and status quo. The family as reproductive unit—re-upping workers for capitalism's existence, re-supplying subjects of its oppressive/ repressive hegemony and ontology—becomes subverted by the assimilation of taboo as moral standard. An increase in capitalist productivity—what I will call object-productivity—means a deterritorialization of the worker from the workplace—Norman's unvisited motel as pleasure-principle prosthesis, Leatherface's dream/ nightmare house of cannibalistic production, Bertrand as inverted agent of capitalist power, Grossmann, Denke, Haarmann, and Kürten's unemployment and/or work as butchers. (In their occupation as soldiers and/or butchers, Bertrand and the others are employed in professions of suspended taboo.) Bates's repressed sexuality and childlike innocence, Leatherface's retardation and muteness, Bertrand's obsession, the Weimar killers' disenfranchisement, all point to an inherent otherness directly opposite normal social experience and behaviour. Bertrand's transgression of taboo the more extreme as he—as a sergeant—embodies the protective agent of economic and political control. The transgressions of Bates, Leatherface, Bertrand, Kürten and co., evident in their relationships with animals—evisceration (Norman's taxidermy), mutilation (Bertrand's pubescent experiments), bestiality (Kürten's goats and sheep), object-productivity (the work of the butcher)—represent a break with taboo formation. Once taboos are instilled, humans separate from the animal; once transgressed, the transgressor makes a return to the animal—the unrestrained violence, the sex, the death. These transgressors commit necrophilia, necrophagy, and necrosadism as a means of reproducing the initial breaking of a taboo. Their means of production is death, a perverse anti-capitalism, an eroticism of entropy and annihilation.

The sound of grunting, metal in earth and on stone, the eroticized exertion of the exhumation, the black sheet of night covering the ingress until flashbulbs pornographize the bodies— close ups of deliquescing flesh, bones protruding through rotting skin, phallus penetrating vagina, phallic fingers and toes through vaginal mouths and eye sockets, the decomposing flesh wet as if oiled for lubrication. A human face, mouth open, teeth exposed— the agony and the ecstasy. These are close-ups of bodies dug from graves. A cemetery—in the middle, two exhumed bodies posed on a tombstone in sexual congress. At home in both *Psycho* and *The Texas Chain Saw Massacre*, the killer had preserved the body of a mother. Writers Robert Bloch and Thomas Harris, and directors Alfred Hitchcock, Tobe Hooper, and Jonathan Demme, used as their inspiration for Norman Bates, Leatherface (including his extended family), and Jame 'Buffalo Bill' Gumb, the true story of one of the twentieth century's most infamous necrophiles—Ed Gein.

Jame 'Buffalo Bill' Gumb sits in the lip of a deep well in the basement of his house. At the bottom of the well, is a senator's daughter—Catherine Martin—whom he has kidnapped. His plan is to starve her until her skin becomes loose, flay her and use her skin as part of a bodysuit in order to enact a sex change denied to him by the medical profession. 'Jame Gumb: It rubs the lotion on its skin. It does this whenever it's told.

Catherine: Mister, my family'll pay cash. Whatever ransom you're asking for, they'll pay it. Jame Gumb: It rubs the lotion on its skin or else it gets the hose again. (DOG BARKS) Yes, it will, Precious. It will get the hose.'[135]

Three years after the release of *The Silence of the Lambs*, in the English town of Gloucester, police arrested Fred West on the suspicion of kidnap and murder, eventually charging him and his wife Rose with 12 and 10 murders respectively. The West's used their victims as sex slaves before killing them. In *Happy Like Murderers*, Gordon Burn writes, 'All through his [Fred's] life he would invest his deepest and most complicated emotions—all his most difficult and disturbing thoughts—not in people, but in things. Places and things. People as things. He always preferred inanimate objects to breathing, responding—and therefore threateningly dangerous and unpredictable—people. The deadened and dehumanized over the alive and responding. That would be his choice every time.'[136]

Dehumanization, the reduction of the human to the thing, the it, the sex tool, the utensil, an ontic nullity that may be either machine-like—Gumb, West and Gein—or fetishistic—West and Gein. To Gumb, animals are 'Precious' (the name of his poodle), yet human beings are 'its'; for West, tools had personal pronouns—she, he, while humans became 'its'. For Gein, humans became tools, decorations, furniture. Gumb transforms humans into tools for gender reassignment, West turned them into paralyzed sex machines, while Gein made humans into representations of his dead mother and into kitchen utensils. Bertrand viewed humans as organs devoid of any human system—the dead bodies are anti-locomotive, anti-nutritious, and anti-reproductive. West found it difficult to get an erection unless surrounded by tools—hammers, knives, wrenches; Bertrand and Gein had to reduce the 'other' to a 'thing,' to a tool. 'Things themselves are actants—not signifieds, phenomena, or tools for human praxis … Once things are reduced to nothing, they beg you to be conscious of them and to colonize them. Their life hangs by nothing more than a thread, the thread of your attention … Without you the "world," as you put it, would be reduced to nothing.'[137]

West and Gein's murder victims and Bertrand and Gein's exhumed bodies become actants in the consciousness of and colonization by their violent others. Before they become a (dead) signified, a phenomena, a tool for human sexual praxis, they give their existence, their being, to the violent other. In *The Texas Chain Saw Massacre*, Sally Hardesty begs the family not to kill her, saying, 'Please, I'll do anything... anything you want.' Sally will do anything. After being bound, gagged, subjected to sexual violence by Rose and Fred West, and then raped by Fred when Rose leaves the room, Caroline Raine promised not to tell Rose in exchange for her life. Fred agreed and Caroline joined the Wests for the rest of the day, looking after the children, going to the laundrette, before making her escape. From sex slave to economic slave, the women became things of barter, their bodies used in an erotic economics of ontological exchange—a translation of being for existing.

In the opening scenes of *Ed Gein: The Butcher of Plainfield* (2007)—as in *The Texas Chan Saw Massacre*—the audience is privilege to death and distress through flashes in a wider darkness, iterating Nabokov's claim that, 'The cradle rocks above an abyss, and common sense tells us that our existence is but a brief crack of light between two eternities of darkness.'[138] Eventually, a woman appears, rather than hanging by a thread she is suspended by the skin on her back on meat hooks (in a similar manner to Pam in *Chain Saw*). Later in the film, which bears little resemblance to the person of Ed Gein or the violence he committed, detectives discover the flayed skin of Sue Layton (based on Gein's actual victim Mary Hogan) displayed as a fetish/ornament. In a barn adjacent to the house, police also discover the body of Vera Mason (the victim Bernice Worden), her body field dressed as if she were a shot deer. For Gein, these bodies were at once things/ fetishes and consumables. As a hunter would dress a deer in order to preserve meat, so Gein de-organized the corpse, flaying its skin in order to dress himself as a woman—Thomas Harris lifted Buffalo Bill's desire for gender reassignment directly from Ed Gein's profile.

7

NecroAmerica

In reality, the local sheriff, Arthur Schley, entered a remote farmhouse on November the 17th, of 1957. With no electricity, the generator not working, the house dark and stinking of rotten food and rubbish, Schley made his way with trepidation through the rooms, tripping over discarded junk and garbage left to decompose. This was the house of Ed Gein, a local handyman and suspect in a robbery in the nearby town of Plainfield. Bernice Worden, 50-year-old proprietor of the hardware store was missing, Ed had visited the store the night before asking about the cost of antifreeze. The next day, investigating the disappearance, police found a receipt for a gallon of antifreeze written by Worden for Gein. As Schley played his torch over the farmhouse shed, something rubbed against him.

From the wooden beams above, a corpse—more like the carcass of a deer—swung in the frigid yet fetid air, tied upside down to a crossbar, sliced from the genital area through the abdomen to the neck, headless and gutted—the body of Bernice Worden. When more police arrived to assist the sheriff, they discovered her head made into a strange fetish, her heart in a cooking pan on the stove, and yet more items with a gruesome provenance. Human skull bowls, an armchair with a cover made from stitched together human skin, lampshades and baskets also made from skin, women's genitalia salted and kept in a box as if they were Christmas decorations, nipples strung together to make a belt. Where most people would keep snowdomes, potpourri, and china pigs, Gein kept human heads, noses, and a heart. Police also found nine death masks and a suit made from the flayed flesh of women. What had happened to Ed Gein to turn him into a ghoul? What placed him on a par with the skinufacturers of Buchenwald who may have made items from human skin twelve years earlier?

Born on the 27th of August 1906 in La Crosse, Wisconsin, Edward Theodore Gein was the youngest son of parents Augusta and George and brother of Henry. Augusta controlled the family with a strict Lutheran religious moral code, enforced by daily bible studies, visions of hell and severe warnings about the corruptibility of the city, the world, and its women. To Augusta, men were weak, prone to sin and lazy, and she instilled in the boys—particularly Ed—a righteous mistrust of alcohol, sex, and other people. After running a successful grocery store, Augusta moved her family to the country, a rural paradise separate from the flesh of the city and its whirlpool of sin and vice. Gein's father worked as a tanner and some-time carpenter and was (like Kürten's father) a violent alcoholic when home.[139]

The director Joseph Losey was born in La Crosse three years after Ed Gein. In 1951, he directed a remake of Fritz Lang's *M*, this was six years before Gein's police discovered Gein's horror house. Gein probably knew nothing of Kürten and co., but in the year his fellow La Crossean used the basement, staircases, and rooftop of the Bradbury Building in Los Angeles (a precursive psychological architecture to Hitchcock's *Psycho*), Gein was dressing as his mother in a suit he had made from body parts.

The village closest to the 160-acre farm was Plainfield, near to the city of Berlin, Wisconsin. From 1914, the boys attended the local schools where fellow students bullied the shy and bookish Ed because of his effeminate manners and mummy's boy behaviour. His mother would not allow him to make friends, suspicious as she was of anyone outside of the family, and would scold the boys, accusing them of behaving like their no-good, alcoholic father. Ed worshipped his mother and drifted into a lonesome life stirred only by the books he read and the singular company of his older brother.

Their father died of a heart attack in 1940, and the two Gein boys worked as handymen in Plainfield and on the local farms. Although they considered Ed somewhat strange emotionally and socially, the residents trusted him enough to allow him to look after their children. Ed did not mix with others, spending most of his time with his mother; even his brother thought this odd and chastised Ed for his neediness. The area in which they lived was prone to brushfires and on the 16th May 1944, one such fire was burning perilously close to the Gein farm and Ed and Henry went out to battle it. In the smoke, confusion, and encroaching night, Ed could not find Henry. The next day with the fire stifled, Ed reported the disappearance of his brother to the local police. Officers soon found Henry's body in a location shown to them by Ed. Despite some suspicion—the ground around the body was unaffected by the fire, and there was some cranial bruising— police thought the shy and effeminate Ed incapable of murder and the coroner judged the cause of death to be smoke inhalation. With Henry gone, it was just Ed and his mother. But soon after, his mother suffered a series of paralyzing strokes. Gein nursed her for 19 months until, five weeks after the Nuremberg trials began in Germany, on December 29 1945, Augusta died. Throughout Gein's care his mother had verbally abused him.

Ed was devastated yet determined to remain on the farm, eking out an existence through the small amounts of cash he could get as a handyman and babysitter. When the government paid him a subsidy for a soil conservation project, he no longer had to find work and only visited Plainfield for supplies. His mother's rooms on the upper floor—the arena of the superego, Augusta's world of orders, perpetually bombarding Ed with impossible orders, inapplicable ethics, unrealizable morals—was sealed off, as was the downstairs parlour and living room—the realm of the ego, the reality principle. With his mother gone, he no longer had a conception of self, no 'ideal ego,' which is, as Žižek explains it: 'the idealized self-image of the subject (the way I would like to be, I would like others to see me).'[140] Gein's mother—'the Ego-Ideal [is] the agency whose gaze I try to impress with my ego image, the big Other who watches over me and propels me to give my best, the ideal I try to follow and actualize'—was gone, only the id survived free of the superego, the 'agency in its revengeful, sadistic, punishing, aspect.' Ed, alone on his farm, amid the memories of his dead mother, the growing squalor, was living in a Lacanian triad of the Imaginary, the Symbolic, and the Real. 'His own ideal ego is imaginary,' he was his own '"small other," the idealized double-image of his ego,' the retarded handyman, the village idiot, the weirdo in the dark farmhouse out in the woods. Ed's 'ego-Ideal is symbolic, the point of [his] symbolic identification, the point in the big Other' (big mother) from which he observes (and judges) himself; his 'superego is real, the cruel and insatiable agency which bombards [him] with impossible demands and which mocks [his] failed attempts to meet them, the agency in the eyes of which [he is] all the more guilty, the more [he tries] to suppress [his] "sinful" strivings and meet its demands.' With his big mOther dead, he attempted to stifle the cravings of the id (he lived in the basement) and the shouts from the cellar by recreating his mother, by dressing in her very skin, and he did this by raiding graveyards and by murder.

Ed enjoyed reading magazines like *Adventure*, which ran stories such as 'The End of the World' by Franklin Gregory, 'Xipe the Skinless' by Gordon MacCreagh, 'Headhunters of Luzon' by John D. Fawcett, 'Six Under the Earth' by Roaldus Richmond, and 'Human Bloodhounds' by Robert Monroe. His grip on reality weakened by his mother's death and heightened by his solitude, he became addicted to this type of magazine and its tales of Nazi experiments, cannibals, and zombies. He may have even read the ghosted 'The Secret of Elena's Tomb' and Robert Bloch's 'The Mad Scientist' in *Fantastic Adventures* both published in September 1947. He also read books on human anatomy and scoured obituaries in the local newspapers. If the adventure stories and tales of human experiments stimulated his imagination, then the obituaries gave him the time and place to live out his fantasies.

Gein's primary desire was to be a woman, to replace his mother in the mirror, to become mOther in order not to be, to castrate himself, replacing the fatherly Gein for the gynaecological, transferring Gein to Gyne. A bachelor and probably a virgin, Gein had long considered penile amputation as a step towards becoming a woman. On the 1st of December 1952 the New York Daily News ran the headline 'Ex-GI Becomes Blonde Beauty,' regarding Christine Jorgenson (once George Williams Jorgenson, Jr.), famous for undergoing hormone replacement therapy and sex reassignment surgery. Gein read the reports avidly. However, he had found alternative (and less costly) ways to live out his fantasy. Using obituary notices as his guide, in the years after his mother's death, Gein broke into over 40 local graves and tombs, stole female corpses (the majority of women the same age as his mother at her death), or parts of the bodies. He would then take them back to the farm to make household objects from them—turning them into fetishes—and he would use them or wear them. He would scalp a corpse and wear the hair on his head, or peel off the facial skin and wear it as a mask. After carefully cutting away the breasts and attaching them to his chest, he would sit in front of a mirror looking at his transformation. Genitalia excised from the corpses would be worn with his penis and testicles tucked out of sight between his thighs.

Gein's transvestite/ transsexual necrophilia escalated but he found bodies harder to find. On the 8th of December 1954, 51-year-old Mary Hogan went missing from a tavern she ran in Pine Grove. A trail of blood and a cartridge from a .32-caliber pistol were found in the bar but, although Gein was suspected, no evidence could be found to arrest him for the woman's disappearance. Three years later, Gein's .32 pistol would be found by police investigating the death of Bernice Worden.

Technically, Gein was not a serial killer, having been charged with only two killings—Mary Hogan and Bernice Worden. Found by psychologists and psychiatrists to be a sexual psychopath, mentally unfit to stand trial, on the 16th of January 1958, he was moved to the Central State Hospital for the Criminally Insane at Waupun, Wisconsin. Ten years later, Gein—judged sufficiently sane by the hospital authorities—stood trial for the two murders. Found guilty but legally insane, the judge sent him to the Mendota State Hospital in Madison, Wisconsin, where he remained until dying there on 26 July 1984.

Gein denied that he had had sex with the corpses, saying that he used them only to satisfy his desire to be a woman. He did, however, sexually mutilate the bodies, cutting off their breasts and genitalia and caressing the skin. Gein's necrophilia shares common areas of paraphilia with Bertrand—mutilation and possible incestuous, mother-dominated sexuality. But, whereas Bertrand revelled in the decomposition and viscera of the bodies, Gein was repulsed by their smell. He was more fascinated with the surface appearance of the skin as a means to replace his mother. He enjoyed the sensation of flaying the dead bodies. Maybe this had something to do with his father's work as a tanner. Where Bertrand had sex with the internal organs, Gein pickled them or kept them in the refrigerator. Where Bertrand enacted a power over the dead bodies, Gein attempted to cloak himself in a woman's power. Both men claimed to be dazed or 'not themselves' when defiling the graves and bodies, and both men related their crimes without emotion or remorse. Police found the body parts of ten different women on the farm, eight of these taken from graves and made into fetishes. When his farm and belongings were put up for auction, his car, furniture and other objects became macabre-crime fetish objects,

"Do you know what Ed Gein said about women?"

"Ed Gein?" one of them asks. "Maitre d' at Canal Bar?"

"No," I say, "Serial killer, Wisconsin in the fifties. He was an interesting guy."

"You've always been interested in stuff like that, Bateman," Reeves says, and then to Hamlin, "Bateman reads these biographies all the time: Ted Bundy and Son of Sam and Fatal Vision and Charlie Manson. All of them."

"So what did Ed say?" Hamlin asks, interested.

'"When I see a pretty girl walking down the street I think two things. One part of me wants to take her out and talk to her and be real nice and sweet and treat her right."' I stop finish my J&B in one swallow.

"What does the other part of him think?" Hamlin asks tentatively.

"What her head would look like on a stick."[141]

For Bertrand, West, Gein, Kürten, and co., women's bodies, in differing stages of peri-mortal being, became desiring machines, autonoma, tools, revivified objects of control even within and beyond the acts of desecration, defilement, and murder. To Bertrand, women's bodies were organ bundles, linked signifying chains of desire; devoid of a self, a conscious, they became partial objects. For Bertrand, 'repulsion is the condition of the machine's functioning, but attraction is the functioning itself.'[142] When West took the phalanges, metacarpals, patellas, the scapulas of his victims as trophies (these have never been found), he was taking the tool organism/ machine of a human being, its ratchet and screwdriver, its hammer and nails, its hinge and joists. Once Gein had peeled the body to make his mOther costume, he felt the potential of 'becoming–another-sex, the becoming-god, the becoming-a-race, etc.'[143] All necro-agents were 'forming zones of intensity on the body without organs,' for 'every intensity controls within its own life the experience of death, and envelops it.' In Bertrand's flight to the hospital, West's suicide, Gein's acceptance, and Kürten's capture 'it is doubtless the case that every intensity is extinguished at the end, that every becoming itself becomes a becoming-death.'[144]

Bertrand's bodies with organs without, West's bodies as organs, Gein's bodies without organs, and Kürten's body as an organ of society, conglomerate into a compacted alien-organsism, something close to the being in John Carpenter's *The Thing*, beyond life and yet inclusive of everything it touches, a being irrepresentable in the imagination, 'a notion of Thing as an Id-Machine, a mechanism that directly materializes our unacknowledged fantasies.'[145]

Where Bertrand was fascinated by human organs, Gein made objects out of them, and West manipulated them into organami, de-articulatung bodies to fit a set space. Where Bertrand and Gein deterritorialized bodies from their places of internment, West and another probable necrophile—John Reginald Halliday Christie—interritorialized in their family's living space, a house, a '"group of organic habits," or even something deeper, the shelter of the imagination itself.'[146]

8

NecroBritannia

In June 1937, seven years after the execution of Peter Kürten, and seven years before the death of Ed Gein's mother, John Reginald Halliday Christie and his wife moved to North Kensington, London. Their home—a prototypical 25 Cromwell Street—comprised the ground-floor flat and garden at 10 Rillington Place, an end-terrace Victorian property in a cul-de-sac surrounded by factories and train lines. The three-storey house contained two more apartments (they originally moved into the top-floor flat, later home to the Evanses), basic sanitation, and an outdoor toilet. John Christie was born in 1898 in Halifax, Yorkshire. His father physically abused him as a child (see Kürten and Gein), his mother mollycoddled him (see Gein), and his four sisters taunted and bullied him for his effeminacy, hypochondria, and fear of dirt—he suffered from automyso-phobia (fear of being dirty) and mysophobia (fear of dirt). And it was his sisters that formed his first erotic memories (see Kürten), these may also have stemmed from memories of his maternal grandfather's funeral (another man whom he feared) at which he felt release at the sight of the dead body. He later invented games in which he would explore children's tombs in the local graveyard (Gein and Bertrand).

Although he bragged about his sexual conquests, Christie was known to have a very small penis. He found it difficult to fully satisfy women and became impotent at the thought of their rejection. He lost his voice for three years after being struck by a mustard-gas shell during service in the First World War. Psychiatrists believed this to be a hysterical reaction—an embedded fear that manifested itself in a hypochondriacal silence—caused by the horror of the trenches, the half-buried bodies in the sickening mud. Christie could have been the anti-hero of Wilfred Owen's 'The Dead-Beat.'

> He dropped, — more sullenly than wearily,
> Lay stupid like a cod, heavy like meat,
> And none of us could kick him to his feet;
> Just blinked at my revolver, blearily;
> – Didn't appear to know a war was on,
> Or see the blasted trench at which he stared.
> "I'll do 'em in,' he whined, "If this hand's spared,
> I'll murder them, I will."
> A low voice said, "It's Blighty, p'raps, he sees; his pluck's all
>   gone, Dreaming of all the valiant, that AREN'T dead:
> Bold uncles, smiling ministerially;
> Maybe his brave young wife, getting her fun
> In some new home, improved materially.
> It's not these stiffs have crazed him; nor the Hun."
>
> We sent him down at last, out of the way.
> Unwounded; — stout lad, too, before that strafe.
> Malingering? Stretcher-bearers winked, "Not half!"
>
> Next day I heard the Doc.'s well-whiskied laugh:
> "That scum you sent last night soon died. Hooray!"

After leaving the army, Christie worked in an office and, in 1920, married Ethel Simpson Waddington. He used prostitutes to fulfil his sexual fantasies but they often taunted him with his lack of sexual prowess—it may have been on these visits that he lived out his erotic dream of an unconscious, malleable, and uncomplaining woman—who would lie 'stupid like a cod, heavy like meat.' Christie worked as a postman in Sheffield during the early years of his marriage but was caught stealing postal orders and sentenced to three years in prison. He returned to the Post Office to work but left after a violent episode.

In 1923, he moved alone to London to look for work but spent nine months in prison for theft. He moved in with a prostitute on his release and was imprisoned for a further six months after assaulting her with a cricket bat. After a further spell in prison for theft, and arrests but no convictions for assaulting women, in 1933, in an attempt to normalize his life, Christie asked his wife to join him in London. After a separation of ten years, Edith soon discovered that life with Christie was anything but normal. After a car accident, which may have been a form of self-assault, Christie's hypochondria metastasized and he plagued doctors and hospitals with minor and imaginary ailments—malingering.

As World War Two began, Christie somehow managed to sign up as a War Reserve Police volunteer at Harrow Road Police Station, working there for four years. He could live out his fantasies of power and authority, of stalking and voyeurism. Like Fred West, he made a spy-hole in a door to watch sexual activity; like Kürten, he followed and befriended women; like Gein, he became eroticized by bodily trophies. And—like Ted Bundy 30 years later—he became something of a ladies' man and was once caught and beaten by a jealous husband. Rather than risk a repeat thrashing—his pluck's all gone—Christie decided to use his new home as his erotic space, his necrotic arena.

An archetypal Foucauldian poweroticist, Christie pretended to be a doctor, a medic, or to have license as a policeman to enact scientific disciplines—and so knowledge and domination—on his subjects (women) who became objects within the medicinal/ control unconscious/ power sexual act. If 'sex is placed by power in a binary system: licit and illicit, permitted and forbidden,'[147] then Christie eventualized this binary system as thief/ police husband/ trick John/ john.

In August 1943, with his wife away in Sheffield, Special Constable Christie met Ruth Fuerst in a local pub—the Elgin Arms or the Kensington Park Hotel. Ruth, 21, an Austrian by birth, worked in the James Bartle Western Iron Works on Lancaster Road behind Rillington Place. Ruth may have augmented her wages by working as a prostitute to pay for her single room. She visited Christie whenever his wife left for Sheffield. One night, Christie strangled her during sex claiming—as Fred West would about the death of Lucy Partington 30 years later—that Ruth wanted him to leave his wife for her. In West's words he strangled her 'when "she come the loving racket" and was threatening to tell Rose about their affair.'[148] Likewise, Christie—in fear of his wife discovering the affair—strangled Ruth in bed while having pre-, peri-, and post-mortem sex. Afterwards, he used her leopard-print coat to wrap her excrement and urine-stained body and, again like West's first Cromwell Street murder, placed her under floorboards in the front parlour—West used the bathroom. Christie's wife and her brother returned later that day unaware of what had occurred. Again, like West, when Christie had the opportunity, he removed the body and hid it in the garden washhouse. Unlike West, Christie's wife knew nothing of his predilections and interrupted his plans to rebury the corpse. He had to wait until nightfall to dig a suitable hole in the garden, interred the body with a bundle of Ruth's clothes, and burned other articles belonging to her. Later the next year, while gardening, he unearthed the skull and put it in the rubbish to go to the incinerator.

Christie, Gein, and West invested their 'deepest and most complicated emotions—all [their] most difficult and disturbing thoughts—not in people, but in things. Places and things'[149]—so 10 Rillington Place, the Plainfield farmhouse, 25 Cromwell Street; Christie's simulated medical apparatus, Gein's skinufactured kitchenware and clothing, West's tools, But whereas Bertrand, Gein, and West claimed to have a hazy recollection of events, Christie's use of power as erotics caused an inner calm, he wrote in his memoirs, 'I remember, as I gazed down at the still form of my first victim, experiencing a strange, peaceful thrill.'[150]

Killing women by strangulation would be the only way Christie could achieve orgasm.

To his Notting Hill neighbours, Christie and his wife appeared a normal if somewhat private couple, they kept pets and Christie became involved in local sports activities and joined the local choir. But when his wife travelled north, Christie would seek opportunities to kill. After resigning his volunteer commission in the War Reserve Police, Christie started work at Ultra Radio Works in nearby Acton. In the firm's canteen, he met 32-year-old Muriel Eady. Rather than re-enacting the opportunist lust murder of Ruth Fuerst, Christie carefully planned his next sex killing. With Edith visiting relatives in Sheffield, Christie invited Muriel to 10 Rillington Place in October 1944 in order to 'cure' the bronchitis from which she suffered. Muriel had been to tea on a number of occasions with Edith present.[151]

Like West and Gein, Christie feared violent physical confrontation and sought a method to incapacitate his victim. West would knock the women unconscious and then bind them with packing tape, Gein shot his victims and then strung them up. Christie constructed an inhaler, an appliance made from a jar filled with Friar's Balsam (a non-prescription inhalent), and a cut length of hosepipe leading to the gas supply, the balsam disguised the smell. After a cup of tea, Muriel inhaled the mixture. The coal gas contained 15% carbon monoxide and soon made Muriel dizzy, weakening her enough for Christie to use a stocking to strangle her and had intercourse with her as she died. Afterwards, he carried her body to the washhouse, dug a grave, and buried her in the garden close to the body of Ruth Fuerst. Again, while gardening a little later, he uncovered a femur and — in a manner Fred West would have approved of — he used it to jack up the garden trellis. Like Gein and West, Christie took something from the bodies as a power trophy, a sexual and hiero-phantic fetish, a means of reliving the erotic and necrotic event, relieving the tension, and re-enlivening his fantasies.

Six years later, on 14 December 1952, Christie killed his wife. While she was asleep, he strangled her with a stocking. After three days, he wrapped her in a blanket and buried her under the floorboard in the front parlour. Later, he would tell police he had killed her as an act of mercy as she asphyxiated in a suicide attempt, driven to it by the new West Indian neighbours. Christie wrote to her relatives explaining that Ethel had been invalided by rheumatism; he told neighbours she had moved back to Sheffield or was living in Birmingham. He pawned her jewellery, sold the furniture, and illegally withdrew funds from her bank account. With his wife dead, Christie's lust murders increased and intensified.

When caught, Christie—despite his meticulous planning and obsessive-compulsive traits—appeared confused as to the order of the killings. Police and forensic evidence suggest that he killed 25-year-old Rita Nelson soon after the death of his wife. At some point towards the end of January 1953, Christie claimed the six-month pregnant Rita verbally abused him in the street, threatening to go to the police and have him arrested for violence if he did not pay her 30 shillings. He then attested she barged into his house, attempted to assault him with a frying pan, and that he grabbed her and knocked her to the floor. According to Christie (in a similar manner to Bertrand, Gein, and West) he had blacked out and, on regaining consciousness, found that he had strangled her with a rope. He retired for the night. The next morning, he cleaned away the excrement, urine, and blood, and placed the body in a cupboard. The police and Christie's biographer Ludovic Kennedy theorized that he met her in a local pub. Rita asked him to abort her unwanted child and he invited her back to the house to perform the operation.

A week before he strangled his wife, Christie had met 26-year-old prostitute Kathleen Maloney and had taken pornographic photographs of her and her friend. In February, soon after strangling and raping Rita Nelson, Christie met Kathleen in the San

Remo café on Lancaster Road. Again he claimed he had no memory of killing her and that he found the body and stored it in the cupboard next to Rita. He later admitted using a device similar to the gas/ balsam inhaler to render her unconscious before strangling and raping her. He appeared to be gaining some epistemological furtherance to the biomechanics of death by placing a diaper under her to soak up the blood, excrement, and urine. Rather than fit her into the cupboard, he left the corpse sitting in a chair and had breakfast with it the next morning before covering the body in a blanket, fitting a pillowcase over the head, and then entombing it in the cupboard under dirt and dust from the garden.

Christie boasted about his medical prowess in the local pubs and cafés, and propositioned a few women promising cures for migraine, asthma, and offering backstreet abortions. On the 6th of March 1953, Christie met 26-year-old Hectorina McLennan, she lived with her boyfriend in an unfurnished flat near to Rillington Place. Christie, being the good neighbour, invited her around for tea. He later admitted to police that he had struggled with her, ripped off her clothes, and she had passed out. But police discovered he had used gas, strangled her, and raped her as she died. Hectorina joined Rita and Kathleen in the cupboard. Both 10 Rillington Place and 25 Cromwell Road became necrophiliac spaces, dead rooms within the living space, similar to Gregor Schenider's *Totes Haus UR* (*The Dead House*), in which rooms are made smaller to incorporate other rooms invisible to the viewer. There are rooms called Last Hole, Totally Insulated Guest Room, The Smallest Wank, Large Wank and Love nest. Crawl spaces are littered with clothing, a deflated sex dolls, magazines. Schneider had started work on *Haus UR*, the forerunner to The Dead House, in 1985, at a time when the Wests' Cromwell Road house held similar uncanny and hidden rooms and bodies.

Christie moved out of 10 Rillington Place two weeks later. The new resident discovered the bodies while fixing a bracket to the wall and inadvertently breaking through it. Police later unearthed the bodies of Ruth, Muriel, and Edith in the garden.

Four years earlier, in 1949 they had found another two bodies, those of Beryl Evans and her 13-month-old baby Geraldine, both of whom had been strangled and wrapped in blankets. They had lived in the top floor flat of 10 Rillington Place and Beryl's husband and Geraldine's father Timothy Evans had been hanged for their murders on the 9th of March 1950, Christie giving evidence for the prosecution. The autopsy team had found evidence of vaginal bruising and attempts at post-mortem sexual intercourse with Beryl's body but this was not presented to the court. Commentators disagree on what really happened, and there are various theories as to who murdered Beryl and Geraldine.

Of the six bodies discovered in the house, three had been gassed, strangled and sexually assaulted peri- and/or post-mortem. Two of the bodies found in the garden were identified as the missing persons Ruth Fuerts and Muriel Eady, but their skeletons –dispersed around the garden—could offer no more forensic evidence. The remains of Edith Christie showed that she had been strangled but not gassed or sexually assaulted. Charged only with the murder of his wife, the court and jury found John Reginald Halliday Christie guilty of murder. Albert Pierrepoint—the UK's official executioner—hanged him on July 15 1953. 'That scum you sent last night soon died. Hooray!'

While searching the house, police discovered a tobacco tin holding a collection of female pubic hair—only one batch matched that found on the bodies in the cupboard. Colin Wilson wrote, 'John Christie killed girls for sexual purposes—he seems to have been impotent if the woman was conscious—and walled them up in a cupboard in his kitchen. The cupboard is somehow a symbol of this type of crime—the place where skeletons are hidden by people who are anxious to appear normal and respectable.'[152] He went on to argue that, 'It became clear at the trial that Christie was a necrophile; a woman had to be dead—or at least unconscious—before he could achieve an erection ... the crimes were the outcome of the conflict between the craving for 'primacy'—the desire to be a 'somebody'—and his total lack of sexual self-confidence.'[153] Christie, Gein, and later West, strived for primacy and privacy, primacy over their sexual objects and privacy from the social. Gein disinterred bodies and then reinterred them in his farmhouse. West buried bodies in small holes dug to snugly fit the de-articulated corpses. Christie abandoned the garden for a cupboard, an 'intimate space, space that is not open to just anybody.'[154] For Christie, Gein, and West, their confined spaces (drawers, wardrobes, cupboards, etc,) were 'centers of order that protect(ed) the entire house against uncurbed disorder.'[155] They used these spaces to protect their conscious minds from what they had done. These homicidal necrophiles created arenas in which they could kill without putting themselves at risk. All were inadequate men, cowards, stripped of any empathetic conscience.

> Immediately he felt his wits escape,
> That flash of sunlight veiled itself in crepe.
> All chaos through his intellect was rolled,
> A temple once, containing hoards of gold,
> By opulence and order well controlled,
> And topped with ceilings splendid to behold.
> Silence and night installed their reign in him.
> It seemed he was a cellar dank and dim,
> To which no living man could find the key...[156]

Gein, Christie, and West felt themselves to be disembodied as they killed, as they had sex with corpses—their wits escaped them, they were driven to perform and driven to do so in secrecy, their necrophiliac chaos enacted in confined spaces, in cellars, tombs, cupboards, to which no one had the key except themselves, all consumed in their act by silence and night, by a post-mortem, post-coital calm and peace, a life once again well controlled.

At least twenty women were tortured and killed by Gein, Christie, and West—the majority of them sexually defiled before, during, and after death. If these three necrophiles used the inner space of tombs, cellars, cupboards, then a man who killed more than 30 women used the open road, public dormitories, and beaches to find, kill, and have sex with his victims.

And from that day a very beast was he.
And while he wandered senseless on his way,
Not knowing spring from summer, night from day...[157]

9

NecroSuperstar

This necrophile had no use for cramped space, for secrecy, had no real fear of capture. If Christie, Gein, and West were secretive, furtive, inadequate men with problems of intimacy and impotency, Ted Bundy[158] was brash, intelligent, and a relentless murderer and necrophile wandering the American landscape desensitized; a desiring machine in pursuit of sex and death, reterritorializing the cellar and the grave from stasis and enclosure into space and movement. Space initiates intimacy, topos becomes an extension of self, even detached intimacy means the other in the 'place' of the self, in place of the self. Movement, being on the road and voyaging, replaces topos with chaos, the self continually reterritorialized in search of the constantly fleeing interchangeable other. Gein used a pick-up truck to transport bodies from the cemetery to the farmhouse; West used vans to transport unconscious yet living women to his cellar. Ted Bundy as the symptom, his Volkswagen as a fetish, an impulse image (a sexual and violent energy), his use of fake plaster casts on his limbs to lure his victims into dis-location, a liminal world between desire and fear, where ultimately the reterritorilization becomes deterritorialization, the locus over-riding the topos. For Bundy, the location of his victim's corpse became a place of sexual fulfilment, a necrophiliac pilgrimage to a place (locus) where he was able to re-enact his desires, relive his power, '"You're looking into their eyes and basically, a person in that situation is God! You then possess them and they shall forever be a part of you. And the grounds where you kill them or leave them become sacred to you and you will always be drawn back to them."'[159]

Like Christie and West, Bundy took trophies from his victims and used them as fetish objects; like Gein, these fetishes were heads or body parts he had amputated. Like West and Christie, Bundy was a thief, a liar, and a voyeur. Like Gein, he was unrepentant. But Bundy wanted more than the release of psycho/sociopathic desires and sexual pressure. Bundy wanted to terrorize the country. Like Charles Manson, (arrested in 1969 for his involvement in the Tate and La Bianca murders)—the same year Bundy admitted to first actualizing his fantasy of kidnap and control, the year he found out the true identity of his mother—Bundy also wanted notoriety and fame.

Before an analysis of Bundy's necrophilia, it is worth quoting Georges Bataille at length: 'Sexual activity, whether perverted or not; the behaviour of one sex before the other; defecation; urination; death and the cult of cadavers (above all, insofar as it involves the stinking decomposition of bodies); the different taboos; ritual cannibalism; the sacrifice of animal-gods; omophagia; the laughter of exclusion; sobbing (which in general has death as its object); religious ecstasy; the identical attitude toward shit, gods, and cadavers; the terror that so often accompanies involuntary defecation; the custom of making women both brilliant and lubricious with makeup, gems and gleaming jewels; gambling, needless expenditure, and certain fanciful uses of money, etc. together present a common character in that the object of the activity (excrement, shameful parts, cadavers, etc.) is found each time treated as a foreign body (*daz ganz Anderes*); in other words, it can just as well be expelled following a brutal rupture as reabsorbed through the desire to put one's body and mind entirely in a more or less violent state of expulsion (or projection). The notion of the (heterogeneous) foreign body permits one to note the elementary subjective identity between types of excrement (menstrual blood, urine, fecal matter) and everything that can be seen as sacred, divine, or marvellous: a half-decomposed cadaver fleeing through the night in a luminous shroud can be seen as characteristic of this unit.'[160]

'The custom of making women both brilliant and lubricious with makeup...' After Bundy had raped and killed the young women, mutilated them, vaginally and anally raped them post-mortem, he would drive away, back into town, to find new victims. But soon after the deaths, he would become consumed with a desire to visit the bodies again, to spend the night with them under the starry skies of Taylor Mountain. He would return, have sex with the bodies, wash their hair, and apply makeup to their faces. Mother destroyed, mother resurrected.

Born on the 24th of November 1946 in Vermont, Theodore Robert Cowell grew up not knowing that his sister Louise was, in fact, his mother and that his parents were actually his maternal grandparents. 'Fear cements his compound, conjoined to another world, thrown up, driven out, forfeited. What he has swallowed up instead of maternal love is an emptiness, or rather a maternal hatred without a word for the words of the father; that is what he tries to cleanse himself of, tirelessly. What solace does he come upon within such loathing? Perhaps a father, existing but unsettled, loving but unsteady, merely an apparition but an apparition that remains. Without him the holy brat would probably have no sense of the sacred; a blank subject, he would remain, discomfited, at the dump for non-objects that are always forfeited, from which, on the contrary, fortified by abjection, he tries to extricate himself. For he is not mad, he through whom the abject exists.'[161]

In 1950, his mother/sister took him to Tacoma, Washington, to live in the home of relatives. One afternoon, his aunt woke after a nap to find herself surrounded by knives, Ted standing beside her smiling.

While in Tacoma, Louise met and married Johnnie Culpepper Bundy, an army cook, and Ted took the man's surname. Despite babysitting for his younger siblings, Ted felt distanced from his new family and spent most of his time alone. Like Gein and Christie, Ted was bullied and teased at school, making him feel like an outsider—'the laughter of exclusion; sobbing (which in general has death as its object)'—inadequate in some way, social stigmatism and sexual doubt combining to create resentment and increased isolation. Despite this social and sexual exclusion, Ted was a straight-A student. This aptitude for learning made him more confident and, at high school, he began to socialize and was considered neat, tidy, and polite but rarely did this translate to having a steady girlfriend. Ted was learning to wear masks. Although his schools and colleges thought him diligent, hard-working, and intelligent, the jobs he held to pay his way through education were short-lived and many—like Christie and West, Bundy was a thief. He spent his free time getting involved in politics, skiing in the local mountains—maybe unconsciously mapping his locus. In an interview with Detective Bob Keppel, Bundy stated, 'It all began in Washington State. That's where I was living, that's where I grew up as a kid … and those kinds of images, impulses, and behaviours which ultimately led to the violent behaviour occurred if you will, in Washington State.'[162]

It was during one of his ski weekends that he met and fell in love with a Californian woman. It is probable that Ted lost his virginity to the woman and became obsessed with her. The feelings were not reciprocated, the young woman thinking Ted rootless and unambitious. To add to his masks, Ted began to lie, invent stories, show off—'gems and gleaming jewels; gambling, heedless expenditure, and certain fanciful uses of money, etc. together present a common character in that the object of the activity (excrement, shameful parts, cadavers, etc.) is found each time treated as a foreign body.' The gambling, gems, and gleaming jewels came in the shape of a scholarship to Stanford, but these turned to excrement and shame as he found himself out of his depths socially, intellectually, and economically at the elite institution.

In his obsession with the young woman's '(heterogeneous) foreign body,' Ted saw 'everything that can be seen as sacred, divine, or marvellous'; however, in 1968, she ended the relationship, leaving Ted devastated, and reliving feelings of inadequacy and doubt, his identity lost in a morass of 'excrement (menstrual blood, urine, fecal matter),' retreating to the elementary subjective identity of his childhood, his loneliness, inauthenticity, abandonment, and socio-sexual alienation. Ted would spend the rest of his life attempting to relive the relationship (they continued to write and meet), to get back with her as well as at her, her rejection of him, an expulsion 'following a brutal rupture as reabsorbed through the desire to put one's body and mind entirely in a more or less violent state of expulsion (or projection)'. The expulsion, reabsorbed through his innate (and repressed) violence, created the need to project his desires on women who resembled the original foreign body—to overcome the exclusion and sobbing, he would begin a simulated 'ritual cannibalism; the sacrifice of animal-gods; omophagia.' He would consume her, burn her, and have sex with her as raw meat in the shape of dead bodies—and then attempt to re-member her, make her new, destruction and reconstruction.

Around this time, Ted also discovered the truth that his sister was his mother, and his parents really his grandparents. His 'heedless expenditure, and certain fanciful uses of money' manifested itself in shoplifting, burglary, and theft for which he felt no remorse, believing he was entitled to whatever he stole using these 'gems and gleaming jewels' to bankroll his perversions. The thrill of thievery, again, made him more confident—like West and Christie, he revelled in getting one over on authority, taking the power, controlling (or so he thought) his life through controlling others.

As part of his mask, his adoption of roles, he studied—and excelled at—psychology at the University of Washington. 'Out of the daze that has petrified him before the untouchable, impossible, absent body of the mother, a daze that has cut off his impulses from their objects, that is, from their representations, out of such daze he causes, along with loathing, one word to crop up—fear. The phobic has no other object than the abject. But that word, "fear"—a fluid haze, an elusive clamminess—no sooner has it cropped up than it shades off like a mirage and permeates all words of the language with nonexistence, with a hallucinatory ghostly glimmer.'[163]

Ted met a woman (usually pseudonymized as Elizabeth Kendall). The relationship was the reverse of Ted's love affair with the Californian woman. Elizabeth wanted to get married, for Ted to be a father figure for her daughter from a previous marriage. Aware that Ted did not have the same feelings—and that he was seeing other women—she waited. In this relatively stable period, Ted became ambitious, applying to law schools and furthering his interest in politics. A Republican, he worked on the Washington governor Daniel J. Evans' re-election campaign, volunteered for a local suicide hotline call centre, and enrolled at the University of Puget Sound law school. This could all have been an elaborate mask, a narrativization of his obsession and jealousy. 'Bataille occasionally discusses more commonplace, though by no means less disturbing, associations of sex and death, for example the association of sexual jealousy or possession with the destructive impulse.'[164]

On a visit to California through the autumn and winter of 1973 with the Washington Republican Party, he went out several times with his ex-girlfriend and successfully rekindled their romance—he had become what she wanted—confident, ambitious, driven. For Ted, this had nothing to do with love and marriage; this had everything to do with power and revenge. This was when the excremental turned sacred, when violence became marvellous, when he could cannibalize and consume the object of his rejection and alienation. In February 1974, he finished the relationship, when the woman called to ask why, he denied knowing her. 'The theory of the unconscious, as is well known, presupposes a repression of contents (affects and presentations) that, thereby, do not have access to consciousness but effect within the subject modifications, either of speech (parapraxes, etc.), or of the body (symptoms), or both (hallucinations, etc.). As correlative to the notion of repression, Freud put forward that of denial as a means of figuring out neurosis, that of rejection (repudiation) as a means of situating psychosis. The asymmetry of the two repressions becomes more marked owing to denial's bearing on the object whereas repudiation affects desire itself (Lacan, in perfect keeping with Freud's thought, interprets that as "repudiation of the Name of the Father").'[165]

Bundy always rejected being his own absent father. He rejected others as his father had rejected him, he repudiated his relationship—he as absent father, she as present/ absent mother. He repressed his affections for the female—females reject, they lie, they repudiate relationships. Like Christie, this manifested in symptoms—Christie's hypochondria, Bundy's affectation of plaster casts. Parapraxes—West's asymmetry, assignment and dis-location of personal and impersonal pronouns, Bundy's legalese. Hallucinations—West, Christie, Gein, and Bundy all describe hallucinatory experiences prior, during, or after their necro-erotic events.

Did Bundy start killing after he gained revenge? Was it the only way he could relive that feeling, that intensity of power? He may have killed as early as 1971, when he was 14. He boasted of killing two women in Atlantic City in 1969 but no bodies were found. It is certain that he practised violence and kidnapping as early as 1969 as a prelude to his homicidal lust murders that began in 1972 and went on (re-hearsing) until his first substantiated murder in 1974. The rapes, kidnappings, and murders had gone undetected, he had exacted revenge on the woman who rejected him. Why would he need a girlfriend/ wife when there were women out there who would not argue, would do whatever he wanted, and would not, eventually, reject him? Bundy's sadism and necrophiliac tendencies were evident, as he actualizes Bataillean moments of necro-erotics. '... the association of sexuality with the desire to kill the 'partner' (the victim, in fact); the 'inauthenticity' and inferiority of shared erotic pleasure; the reduction of the other (invariably a woman) to the level of inert object—Bataille is quite correct in reading Sade as advocating much the same doctrine (Juliette: 268-269). ... Like Sade, Bataille tends to conflate the living with the dead—an 'erotics' that denies the presence of the other person. It is, essentially, masturbatory or even necrophiliac, as neither Sade nor Bataille can distinguish between sex with another person from merely penetrating a cadaver.'[166]

On the 4th of January 1974, a month before he concluded his revenge, Bundy broke into the basement bedroom of a University of Washington student in Seattle. He knocked Joni Lenz (18) unconscious, stripped her and raped her with a speculum. The young woman went into a coma for ten days and suffered internal injuries and permanent brain damage from the attack but survived. This would become only a part of Bundy's modus operandi, to break into apartments—the first rape, the penetration of another's locus, the other's topos—and he would do so late at night, usually after midnight. At about the same time as he denied knowing the woman who rejected him, abjected him, made him abject—from reject, to deject, to abject—he returned to the University of Washington campus, entered the room of 21-year-old psychology major Lynda Anne Healy—a weather announcer for local radio ski information shows—bludgeoned her with a crowbar until she lost consciousness and kidnapped her. The young woman who shared the apartment with Lynda heard nothing until woken by her alarm clock. But Lynda wasn't there, nor was she at work—the radio station had called asking for her. The bedroom looked normal; maybe Lynda had gone for a walk. But when Lynda's parents called to see why she was late for dinner, friends, relatives, and colleagues started to worry and called the police. 'A young girl, a freshman, I met in a bar in Cambridge my junior year at Harvard told me early one fall that "Life is full of endless possibilities." I tried valiantly not to choke on the beer nuts I was chewing while she gushed this kidney stone of wisdom, and I calmly washed them down with the rest of a Heineken, smiled and concentrated on the dart game that was going on in the corner. Needless to say, she did not live to see her sophomore year. That winter, her body was found floating in the Charles River, decapitated, her head hung from a tree on the bank, her hair knotted around a low-hanging branch, three miles away.'[167]

When they arrived, police discovered a small trace of blood on a pillow and on a nightgown. Clothes were missing—a white blouse, jeans, and boots. Police also found an unlocked door but were not certain that any foul play had occurred. 'Instead of sounding himself as to his "being," he does so concerning his place: "Where am I?" instead of "Who am I?" For the space that engrosses the deject, the excluded, is never one, nor homogeneous, nor totalizable, but essentially divisible, foldable, and catastrophic.'[168]

Bundy used places he knew intimately—the Cascades, the university campus, and university housing to infiltrate his victims' home before raping and/or kidnapping them. He rendered them unconscious, disabling their senses, his senses taking over the locus, being in control of place without being in control. At these points, he did not want to ask "Who am I"—he was the reject, the deject, the abject—but he knew where he was, where he would go, what places were safe for him. 'Where am I' was always the place of his revenge, of his lust murders—not the place of his rejection, the homogenous dream of a married couple, the totalizable event of man and wife—but the catastrophic division, the place within which he enfolded his rejection and turned it into revenge. After raping Healy, he strangled and then decapitated her, keeping the head as a trophy. 'Sade, in The 120 Days of Sodom, Juliette and La Nouvelle Justine in particular, insists that the taste for cruelty is shared by all with the strength to express it, and typically describes heterosexual intercourse as ideally involving rape, sadism and murder (writes Sade: "[m]urder is a branch of erotic activity, one of its extravagances."'[169]

Reports started to come into university security and police from female students that a man with a light brown Volkswagen and wearing an arm sling had asked them to help him with various things around the campus. Three women went missing and police had no clues as to their whereabouts. On the 11th of June 1974, student Georgeann Hawkins, went missing from the campus. Police could find no evidence of abduction but the increase in disappearances brought forth witnesses who reported seeing a man in a full-leg plaster cast (common in a ski area) who had asked a number of women to help him carry things to his Volkswagen. Infiltration and inauthenticty—the key elements of Bundy's necro-erotic events. 'A deviser of territories, languages, works, the deject never stops demarcating his universe whose fluid confines—for they are constituted of a non-object, the abject—constantly question his solidity and impel him to start afresh. A tireless builder, the deject is in short a stray. He is on a journey, during the night, the end of which keeps receding.'[170]

Bundy created his own locus, devised the arena of his abductions; a smooth-talker schooled in politics and law, good-looking, he extemporised, creating situations in which trust folded into violence, a woman became an object of disgust in order that the non-object (Bundy) could reject his abjection. Bundy, a tireless builder of scenarios, stories, lies, and myths—re-enacted his kills in order to constantly regain the original rush, the 'one' time he felt whole. He worked at night, he worked at twilight, the liminal hours—and he carried away the bodies, on the road, into the mountains.

Police and media had one clue—all the women had long hair

parted in the middle, were wearing jeans or trousers, were thin, and were white. In September 1974, two bodies matching this description were found by grouse hunters in Lake Samamnish State Park—Janice Ott and Denise Naslund, both of whom had gone missing on the 14th of July. Not much remained of their bodies—vertebrae, a skull, a jaw, hair, and femurs (one extra femur from an as-yet unidentified victim). 'Disintegration—I'm taking it in stride.'[171] During the investigation, police questioned people who were on the lake the day of the women's disappearance and discovered that both Janice Ott and Denise Naslund had helped a man called 'Ted' load a boat on to his car, the man was wearing a plaster cast on his arm. 'He has a sense of the danger, of the loss that the pseudo-object attracting him represents for him, but he cannot help taking the risk at the very moment he sets himself apart. And the more he strays, the more he is saved.'[172]

Bundy's confidence/ arrogance/ desire placed him in danger of apprehension, but the power of his compulsion drove him on, the fear of again losing the 'pseudo-object' that attracted and repelled him forced him to take the risk. As he did so, he became 'Ted'—a self apart, a psychological dislocation. He reinforced his power and his dislocated voyeurism by raping and killing one of the women while the other watched. For Bundy as for Sade and Bataille: 'violence [is] essential to sexual activity. Bataille holds that "[p]hysical erotism has in any case a heavy, sinister quality," … sexuality, when taken to its natural limit, leads to murder, and [that] Sade was the great pioneer who affirmed this "truth."'[173]

On October 27 and Thanksgiving Day 28 November 1974, the bodies of Melissa Anne Smith and Laura Aime, both 17, were discovered—they had been beaten on the head, strangled, raped, and sodomized. Both girls were abducted, taken to another place, and killed. Bundy had moved his lust murders to Utah after enrolling at the University of Utah law school—'the more he strays, the more he is saved.' Between the sexual assault of Joni

Lenz in January and the Thanksgiving Day discovery, Bundy had abducted, raped, and killed Lynda Ann Healy (21), Donna Gail Manson (19), Susan Elaine Rancourt (18), Roberta Kathleen Parks (22), Brenda Carol Ball, Georgeann Hawkins (18), Janice Ann Ott (23), Denise Marie Naslund (19), Nancy Wilcox (16), and Debra Kent (17), and attempted to abduct Carol DaRonch (18) who escaped from his car. 'For it is out of such straying on excluded ground that he draws his jouissance. The abject from which he does not cease separating is for him, in short, a land of oblivion that is constantly remembered. Once upon blotted-out time, the abject must have been a magnetized pole of covetousness. But the ashes of oblivion now serve as a screen and reflect aversion, repugnance. The clean and proper (in the sense of incorporated and incorporable) becomes filthy, the sought-after turns into the banished, fascination into shame. Then, forgotten time crops up suddenly and condenses into a flash of lightning an operation that, if it were thought out, would involve bringing together the two opposite terms but, on account of that flash, is discharged like thunder. The time of abjection is double: a time of oblivion and thunder, of veiled infinity and the moment when revelation bursts forth.'[174]

Within the states of Washington and Utah, Bundy had created a 'land of oblivion.' His blotted-out time, the dislocation of grandmother/ mother/ sister, absent father/ present father/ present grandfather/ absent father, the rejection by and rejection of his would-be wife (sister/ mother) forced a covetousness of nothing, of the sister/ mother/ wife made oblivious. By raping, killing, and dis(re)memebering the victims, he made them filthy and allowed himself to feel—'A sudden impulse and an impossible need—these annihilate the heaviness of the world.'[175] The murders—the flash of light he feels when the need is upon him— brings together the two poles of loved sister/ mother/ wife with the reject/ abject mother/ sister/ wife. The lust murders are discharged in the thunder of the crowbar, the flames of the fires in which he incinerated the skulls. For Ted Bundy, these were moments of revelation freeing himself from repression, rejection, and reduplication. 'But what is primal repression? Let us call it the ability of the speaking being, always already haunted by the Other, to divide, reject, repeat. Without one division, one separation, one subject/ object having been constituted (not yet, or no longer yet). Why? Perhaps because of maternal anguish, unable to be satiated within the encompassing symbolic.'[176]

The encompassing symbolic, ruled by language, the name of the father—Bundy struggled within its order. He used language—manipulation/ trust—as part of his MO. He also used force—power—to incapacitate the Other, so that it could no longer haunt him, no longer cause him 'maternal anguish.'

Elizabeth Kendall read reports of the murders and disappearances and suspected Ted of being involved. In August 1974, she contacted police and told them of her suspicions, even providing photographs of Ted for witness identification, but nothing came of it and detectives never questioned Bundy. Because of his ability to evade capture, like West and Christie, Bundy became God in his own symbolic order. As perilous as his assistance/ confrontation actions were, Bundy evolved even riskier practices to secure a victim.

To embed his new symbolic order, Bundy became his own big Other, reified as an agent of law. On the 8th of November 1974, Bundy told Carol DaRonch (18) that someone had attempted to steal things from her car and that she should accompany him to the mall's parking area. Bundy identified himself as Officer Roseland. Although suspicious, DaRonch agreed to go with him to identify the supposed suspect. In the VW, Bundy tried to subdue her with handcuffs and pulled a gun on her when she screamed. She fought back and somehow got free, flagging down a passing motorist and escaping. Although outwardly calm, Bundy began approaching more women in an attempt to kidnap them. Thinking the Utah state police may have witness reports,

Bundy moved his lust murders to different states.

On January 12 1975, he kidnapped, raped and bludgeoned to death Caryn Campbell (23) in Snowmass, Colorado. When discovered, animals had torn apart the body, so police found little direct evidence. Bundy kidnapped and killed Julie Cunningham (26) in Vail, Colorado on the 15th of March. He moved on to Grand Rapids, Colorado where he abducted Denise Oliverson (25) and then to Idaho where he raped and killed 12-year-old Lynette Culver in May. On 28 June, back in Utah, he kidnapped, raped, and killed Susan Curtis (15). None of the bodies were ever discovered. Bundy hid them in the mountains, in the national parks, in a wilderness of fantasy, and he would return to the bodies, rape them, spend the night with them until the decomposition became too much even for him, and he would leave them to nature, bury them in shallow graves, or throw them in a river.

Bundy depersonalized the women by knocking them unconscious, making them the thing. His actions became a murder of the thing, the death of the suppressed-interiorized other. Žižek, writing on Hegel and Lacan states: '"Death drive" thus stands for the annihilation of the thing in its immediate, corporal reality upon its symbolization: the thing is more present in its symbol than in its immediate reality. The unity of the thing, the trait that makes a thing a thing, is decentred in relation to the reality of the thing itself: the thing must "die" in its reality in order to arrive, by traversing its symbol, at its conceptual unity.[177]

Bundy annihilated the women, he dislocated them from their 'there'—college campus, shopping mall, apartment, concert, meeting—as he did so, they became the symbolic representation of his mOther, the woman/ women who rejected him and therefore thwarted his claim to the name of the father. Bundy never felt guilt because the women were more present as symbols than they were (bodily) existing in the immediate reality of murder, rape, and dismemberment. 'I tried to make meat loaf out of the girl but it becomes too frustrating a task and instead I spend the afternoon smearing her meat all over the walls, chewing on strips of skin I ripped from her body.'[178] He decentred them by de-articulating them, making them silent, making his symbolic all-encompassing. He killed them in order to become whole, to close—for however long it took to split again—that rent between signifier (the 30-40 victims) and signified—the mother, the name of the father.

Bundy had been killing at a rate of one victim a month since January 1974. During July 1975, he may have killed Shelley K. Robertson (24), who went missing on the 1st of July, and whose naked body students found in a mineshaft near Vail in August. He never admitted to the killing and denied any knowledge of the death of Nancy Baird (21), who went missing in Utah in early July, her body has never been recovered. Both bear the hallmarks of a Bundy kidnap, rape, sodomy, and murder. He may have denied involvement because he did not have the opportunity to revisit the bodies, they had not yet traversed the symbolic, had not caused the sense of unity.

Before Bundy could find his next victim, Sergeant Bob Hayward of the Utah police arrested him after a car chase on the 16th of August. When Bundy's VW finally pulled over, Hayward and two other officers searched the vehicle and discovered handcuffs, a ski mask, a crowbar, rope, wire, and an ice pick—Bundy like Gein, Christie and West was a tool-being, beyond, before and besides the human, residing in the interstitial realm between being and nothing. 'I had all the characteristics of a human being—flesh, blood, skin, hair—but my depersonal-ization was so intense, had gone so deep, that my normal ability to feel compassion had been eradicated, the victim of a slow, purposeful erasure. I was simply imitating reality, a rough resem-blance of a human being, with only a dim corner of my mind functioning.'[179] The police immediately arrested Bundy on suspicion of kidnapping, rape, and murder. After weeks of questioning, police needed more evidence. Carol DaRonch and another woman picked out Bundy from a line-up on the 2nd of October and police felt certain they had the killer. Two weeks before this, Bundy's partner Elizabeth Kendall told police all she knew about him, his movements, quirks, and interests. With this information, police put together a psychological profile of Ted. The woman who rejected him/ was rejected by him in turn, Elizabeth Kendall, told police about Bundy's sadomasochistic bondage fantasies and role-playing, his absences on the nights of the murders, the plaster of paris and crutches in his room, and his trips into the lakes and mountains. Not only Kendall betrayed Bundy; his friends came forward with accounts of strange objects seen—pantyhose, handcuffs, plaster casts. Police felt they had enough evidence and, on the 23rd of February, Bundy went to court to face charges of abducting Carol DaRonch.

Aggrawal categorizes Bundy as 'a class IXf necrophile,'[180] one who tortures, mutilates, and rapes both the living body and the dead corpse. Like West, he kept his victims alive to torture them; like Christie and Gein, he had sex with them after death until the decomposition disgusted him. Bundy actualized his incestuous homicidal necrophilia through transference—the victims becoming his mother/ sister his mother/ sister/ wife. Aggrawal speculates as to why Bundy became a necrophile. 'When he was a student at the University of Washington, he began a relationship with Stephanie Brooks [the woman has various pseudonyms in Bundy literature], a fellow university student whom he met in 1967. She was a beautiful and highly sophisti-cated woman from a wealthy Californian family. Ted initially could not believe someone from her "class" would have an interest in an ordinary person like him, but they did have common interests. They both loved to ski and it was during their many ski trips together that he fell in love with her. She was possibly the first woman with whom he became involved with sexually. However, she dumped him later, and Bundy seemed to have been deeply hurt. All his victims looked like her, and it is possible that he was trying to get even with her vicariously by murdering and sexually assaulting women who had her appearance.'[181]

Aggrawal fails to consider that the woman reminded Bundy of his sister/ mother, that he hoped the affair would eventuate in a marriage in which he could be the absent husband/ father/for his sister/ mother. Bundy had—in his own mind—committed two different and destructive acts of incest. 'Incest with the sister and incest with the mother are very different things. The sister is not a substitute for the mother: the one belongs to the connective category of alliance, the other to the disjunctive category of filiation. Incest with the sister if prohibited insofar as the conditions of territorial coding require that alliance not be confounded with filiation; and incest with the mother, insofar as descent within filiation must not be allowed to interfere with ascending lines. That is why the despot's incest is twofold, by virtue of the new alliance and direct filiation. He begins by marrying the sister. But he enters into this endogamous marriage outside the tribe, inasmuch as he is himself outside his tribe, on the outside or at the outer limits of the territory.'[182]

Carol DaRonch testified against Bundy on the 23rd of February 1976, telling the court about her horrific experience. She identified Bundy as 'Officer Roseland.' Bundy denied all knowledge of the woman. After four days, the judge found Bundy guilty of aggravated assault and the court later sentenced Bundy to one to fifteen years in Utah State Prison. Psychologists found no evidence of psychoses, neuroses, drug addiction, or sexual deviancy. They concluded that Bundy feared being humiliated by women. Police, however, believed Bundy had killed numerous times. Searching the VW he had sold just before arrest, they found hair matching that of Caryn Campbell and Melissa Smith, and a crowbar with an edge matching indentations in

Campbell's skull. On the 22nd of October, the authorities charged Bundy with murder and extradited him to Garfield County Jail, near Aspen, Colorado. Bundy dismissed his legal team, and prepared to defend himself—that meant access to the court library, without any physical restraints—for the six months leading to the trial.

Behind a bookcase shielded from guards, Bundy managed to open a second-floor window and jump from it onto the courtyard below. On the 7th of June, Bundy escaped into the streets of Aspen, limping from a sprained ankle, he made his way into the mountains, the wilderness graveyard of his desires. Police used bloodhounds and volunteers to search the area, set up roadblocks, and arranged helicopter flyovers. With maps he had secreted in files, Bundy roamed the area looking for a way to escape, and stole food and clothes from cabins and vehicles. Once again, he felt invincible. Now, he had not only eluded capture, he had escaped from the machinery of the law (of the father). However, despite having a map and knowing the mountains, Bundy became lost until he stole a car and drove back into Aspen for supplies. Police spotted the stolen vehicle and re-arrested him. The court allowed him to continue his defence but he had to wear leg-irons while conducting his research. A flight from the Symbolic into the Imaginary in search of the Real only to be returned to the Symbolic. But then Lacan would argue that 'when law is truly present, desire does not stand up, but that it is because law and repressed desire are one and the same thing.'[183]

Bundy simultaneously worked on his defence while plotting another escape. Other inmates supplied him with a hacksaw blade and Carole Ann Boone smuggled in $500 on various visits. Bundy spent months sawing a hole in his cell's ceiling and losing enough weight to fit through; once he had achieved this, he had access to a space above his cell and from there into the guard areas of the prison. On the 30th of December, the day before the guards were supposed to transfer him to Colorado Springs for the trial, Bundy made a figure of his sleeping self out of books, towels, and files, covered it with a sheet and escaped through his bolt hole, crawled along the space to the guards' quarters, down into a cupboard and through that to freedom. 'There is an idea of a [Ted Bundy], some kind of abstraction, but there is no real me, only an entity, something illusory, and though I can hide my cold gaze and you can shake my hand and feel flesh gripping yours and maybe you can even sense our lifestyles are probably comparable: I simply am not there.'[184] After the car he stole broke down, he hitched a ride through the mountains to Vail where he bussed to Denver and then flew to Chicago. Under the alias of Chris Hagen, Bundy made his way to Tallahassee, Florida and rented a single apartment close to the Florida State University campus.

As in the case of Christie, 'Power is essentially what dictates its law to sex.'[185] Bundy's discourse with the machinery of power, of the law, of the symbolic name of the father, legitimized—to him—his actions. Arrested and imprisoned, he escaped with ease. Beyond the law, the power of the court, and the police, Bundy sublimated his absolute self. His desire for death, for violence, sex, and necrophilia acted as transferences between power and sex.

Foucault offers five principal features of this relationship; a closer look will provide a clue to Bundy's necrophiliac tendencies: 'The negative relation. It never establishes any connection between power and sex that is not negative: rejection, exclusion, refusal, blockage, concealment, or mask. Where sex and pleasure are concerned, power can "do" nothing but say no to them; what it produces, if anything, is absences and gaps; it overlooks elements, introduces discontinuities, separates what is joined, and marks off boundaries. Its effects take the general form of limit and lack.'

To expand a Lacanian pun, Bundy was always/ already a sinthome[186]—an artificial self, an auto-creation. 'It is hard for me to make sense on any given level. Myself is fabricated, an aberration. I am a noncontingent human being. My personality is sketchy and unformed, my heartlessness goes deep and is persistent. My conscience, my pity, my hopes disappeared a long time ago (probably at Harvard) if they ever did exist.'[187] To extend the pun further, he embodied the 'negative relation'—he was not brother/ son, not son/ grandson. He could not name himself in relation to those closest to him—sister/ mother, mother/ grandmother, absent father/ father/ grandfather. Powerless to enact his own selfhood in relation to the Other, Bundy sought power (and identity with his father/ grandfather) by torturing animals (as did West, Bundy, and Dahmer). 'There are no more barriers to cross. All I have in common with the uncontrollable and the insane, the vicious and the evil, all the mayhem I have caused and my utter indifference toward it, I have now surpassed.'[188] Rejected by his sister/ mother and mother/ grandmother, Bundy sought replacements to re-enact the rejection. Coming from a less-than-privileged background, he felt excluded from the world of the university elites. Although he found sex and desire in his relationship with Stephanie Brooks, he sought power in involvement with Republican politics. When Brooks ended the relationship, Bundy refused to accept the decision and continued calling and meeting her until—with his new-found confidence and power from his lust murders—rekindled the relationship but on his terms. 'I'm into, oh murders and executions mostly. It depends.'[189] He did so by use of concealment—he had already raped, sodomized, murdered and dismembered a number of women; and by masks—the ambitious law student rather than feckless dreamer. Bundy ended the relationship with a no, a negation of their relations, a negation of her name and her role as partner/ wife— as sister/ mother. He created a gap between them so that they could not be husband/ wife, he absented himself from any normal power/ sex exchange and created that dynamic within himself. The absence he created became the answer—to continually form the absence of the other (women) by using power and sex to create death, to discontinue life but to have power over it through violence and sex. He socially separated what should be joined—husband/ wife—to rearticulate and then de-articulate the sister/ brother, mother/ son network. He transgressed boundaries that had been marked off—houses, apartments—and reticulated a new topology of desire and violence, sex and power, that would bring him to the limits of humanity, to a risk of self-destruction through his complete lack of a signifier, of his lack of being, buy his constant desire to (*manqué-a-etre*) want-to-be. Bundy's fundamental fantasy was to regain what he lacked—symbolic castration by his absent (castrated) father. He refused to accept that the ultimate sexual object does not exist and looked for it in his victims, believing they embodied the lost object. Bundy wilfully pursued the Other in his attempt to fulfil his desire and fill the absences. He saw the bodies of his victims as the object-cause of his desire, he raped and sodomized them after death—like the Moche of northern Peru circa 100-800 AD—to become immortal, 'We should not forget that the death drive is a Freudian name for immortality, for a pressure, a compulsion, which persists beyond death.'[190] For Bundy, walking through the campus of Florida State University, pressure and compulsion building, he attempted to limit his violent desires, but he could not say no to them.

He could walk the pathways of the leafy campus, check out a few classes, dream that he was back at school. He obtained food, clothes, and electronic equipment by shoplifting or with stolen credit cards. Like Christie before him and West after, Bundy was a consummate and compulsive thief, stealing as a means of going beyond the law in everyday acts, small events that tested his personal power against that of the authority. 'Is evil something you are? Or is it something you do?'[191]

On the 15th of January 1978, around 3am, Bundy broke into the

Chi Omega sorority house of Florida State University. One of the students, Nita Neary, returning after a night out and finding the door open, heard a noise that frightened her. She stepped into the shadows by the staircase and saw a man run down the stairs and into the street:

'Secondly, power prescribes an "order" for sex that operates at the same time as a form of intelligibility: sex is to be deciphered on its relation to the law. And finally, power acts by laying down the rule: power's hold on sex is maintained through language, or rather through the act of discourse that creates, from the very fact that it is articulated, a rule of law. It speaks, and that is the rule. The pure form of power resides in the function of the legislator; and its mode of action with regard to sex is of a juridico-discursive character.'[192]

Bundy spent his childhood in an illicit relationship with his sister/ mother, permitted to have sibling feelings but forbidden to have filial attachments. The binary system of mother/ son sister/ brother confused, unintelligible to the boy, the 'order' of familial power reversed, negated into dual dynamics of sex and loss, love and absence. The rule of law—the mother's and the father's—denied, deflected, withdrawn, transferred—could never implant, the discourse changing constantly. Bundy discovered who he was not at the same time as he found a means of being whole—of possessing discourse—the time he began kidnapping and murdering women in 1961. To regain power (and therefore to have some control over his sex life), he enrolled in law school, joined the Republican Party, and the Church of Jesus Christ of Latter-day Saints, taking on the role of a would-be legislator, a successful lawyer practising juridical discourse.

Nita Neary ran to her room and told Nancy her roommate what she had seen—a man wearing a dark cap carrying what looked like a log wrapped in a blanket. Before they could raise the alarm, they saw one of their friends—Karen Chandler—covered in blood. Nita rushed to the housemother's room and they started to check the rooms. Bundy had bludgeoned Karen Chandler (21) as she slept, breaking her jaw, smashing teeth, injuring her hands, and causing concussion. 'The cycle of prohibition: thou shalt not go near, thou shalt not touch, thou shalt not consume, thou shalt not experience pleasure, thou shalt not speak, thou shalt not show thyself; ultimately thou shalt not exist, except in darkness and secrecy. To deal with sex, power employs nothing more than a law of prohibition. Its objective: that sex renounce itself. Its instrument: the threat of punishment that is nothing other than the suppression of sex. Renounce your self or suffer the penalty of being suppressed; do not appear if you do not want to disappear. Your existence will be maintained only at the cost of your nullification. Power constrains sex only through a taboo that plays on the alterative between two nonexistences.'[193]

Bundy's early fetishes, driven by his feelings of alienation and detachment, were fetishes of prohibition—do not go near (voyeurism) and do not touch (pornography), and his familial relationships mirrored these fetishes—no pleasure, no jouissance because of castration and, therefore, no language with which to understand the experience. Bundy's voyeurism and addiction to pornography created women—the Other—as partial objects upon which he transferred his transgressive enjoyment moving beyond the pleasure principal into pain. He denied his own non-existence as he killed others in the darkness of the night, in the secrecy of their rooms, in the dark secrecy of the mountains. After escaping from prison, these prescriptions meant nothing to Bundy, he had gone beyond the word of the law. Rather than suppress his need for sex, he turned the discourse into an expression of his perversions (his search for the father). Rather than renounce (denounce) himself to the law (to admit his crimes), in the Chi Omega sorority house, Bundy announced himself above the word of the law, became the messenger of his (non)-existence. He appeared—staged an event of brutal sex and violence—and disappeared. Both his existence and the death of the young women creating a double bind of his and their non-existence.

Police arrived at the sorority house and found the body of Margaret Bowman (21), strangled with nylon pantyhose and beaten so severely with a log that her skull had split revealing her brain. They moved on to the next room. Attacked while she slept, Kathy Kleiner (21), suffered cuts to her upper body and a broken jaw from the attack but had survived. 'The logic of censorship. This interdiction is thought to take three forms: affirming that such a thing is not permitted, preventing it from being said, denying that it exists. Forms that are difficult to reconcile. But it is here that one imagines a sort of logical sequence that characterizes censorship mechanisms: it links the inexistent, the illicit, and the inexpressible in such a way that each is at the same time the principle and the effect of the others: one must not talk about what is forbidden until it is annulled in reality; what is inexistent has no right to show itself, even in the order of speech where inexistence is declared; and that which one must keep silent about is banished from reality as the thing that is tabooed above all else. The logic of power exerted on sex is the paradoxical logic of a law that might be expressed as injunction of non-existence, nonmanifestation, and silence.'[194]

Interdiction equals prescription. Before and within language, Bundy was not permitted to be a son, he was prevented from having a mother, saying 'mother,' his mother denied that he existed. He could not reconcile son/ brother, sister/ mother—the principle form of himself had been split, the effect was to deny all others without any censorship mechanisms. The inexistent (either nonexistent or existing totally within himself) fused with the illicit (perversions, fetishes, pornography) to become the inexpressible—necrophilia. Death equalled sex equalled death. As Bundy admitted, in the early stages of his lust murders he killed the women to keep them quiet, to stop them going to the police—to prevent their discourse with power. Bundy obliterated the women, erased their language, and he did so to keep his forbidden actions secret; for them to become a palimpsest on which he could write his own existence; the taboo of necrophilia becoming the manifestation—the roar—of Bundy's being.

Bret Easton Ellis inverts and subsumes Bundy's roar, his desire to keep the mother quiet, to kill the son and become the father, to move within the Real rather than fear the Symbolic. And Ellis creates an Imaginary double—the fissiparous Patrick Bateman. 'Though I am satisfied at first by my actions, I'm suddenly jolted with a mournful despair at how useless, how extraordinarily painless, it is to take a child's life. This thing before me, small and twisted and bloody, has no real history, no worthwhile past, nothing is really lost. It's so much worse (and more pleasurable) taking the life of someone who has hit his or her prime, who has the beginnings of a full history, a spouse, a network of friends, a career, whose death will upset far more people whose capacity for grief is limitless than a child's would, perhaps ruin many more lives than just the meaningless, puny death of this boy. I'm automatically seized with an almost overwhelming desire to knife the boy's mother too, who is in hysterics, but all I can do is slap her face harshly and shout for her to calm down. For this I'm given no disapproving looks. I'm dimly aware of light coming into the room, of a door being opened somewhere, of the presence of zoo officials, a security guard, someone – one of the tourists? – taking flash pictures, the penguins freaking out in the tank behind us, slamming themselves against the glass in a panic. A cop pushes me away, even though I tell him I'm a physician. Someone drags the boy outside, lays him on the ground and removes his shirt. The boy gasps, dies. The mother has to be restrained.'[195]

In an adjacent room to the one in which police found Kathy Kleiner, they discovered the bludgeoned body of Lisa Levy (20). Bundy had strangled her. Police found bite marks on her buttocks, one of her nipples had been scissored by the attacker's teeth and hung from her breast. After she died, Bundy used a hair-spray canister to sexually assault the body. 'The things I could do to you with a coat hanger.'[196] 'The uniformity of the apparatus. Power over sex is exercised in the same way at all levels. From top to bottom in its over-all decisions and its capillary interventions alike, whatever the devices or institutions on which it relies, it acts in a uniform and comprehensive manner; it operates according to the simple and endlessly repro-duced mechanisms of law, taboo, and censorship: from state to family, from prince to father, from the tribunal to the small change of everyday punishments, from the agencies of social domination to the structures that constitute the subject himself, one finds a general form of power, varying in scale alone. This form is the law of transgression and punishment, with its interplay of licit and illicit. Whether one attributes to it the form of the prince who formulates rights, of the father who forbids, of the censor who enforces silence, or of the master who states the law, in any case one schematizes power in a juridical form, and one defines its effects as obedience.'[197]

Bundy had little or no mechanisms of law, taboo, and censorship. No lawgiver to learn from (besides his brutal animal-torturing father/ grandfather); no taboos against pornography, voyeurism, sadomasochism, rape; no censorship of his actions, despite his attempts to fit in and take part. His family—with the blessing of the state—denied him his true existence; his father dis-owned him; school authorities and police—mechanisms of power he needed—ignored evidence that Bundy may have been a thief, kidnapper, rapist, and murderer. Rather than inflict licit punishment, the agencies of social domination allowed Bundy to master and expand his acts of illicit transgression. Bundy became the prince who formulates rights (his law studies and his modus operandi); he had no father who could forbid and so he became the law, the master who made the young women he kidnapped, raped, and killed, obedient to his juridical power—they became his possessions, his effects.

Bundy fled the scene. 'I felt lethal, on the verge of frenzy. My nightly bloodlust overflowed into my days and I had to leave the city. My mask of sanity was a victim of impending slippage. This was the bone season for me and I needed a vacation.'[198] A mile or so away from the sorority house, roommates were woken at 4am by loud noises from the adjoining apartment of their neighbour Cheryl Thomas (21). They called the police, and officers found Cheryl half naked, beaten and bloody, her shoulder dislocated, her jaw broken and her skull fractured in five places. While searching the apartment, they found a mask by the bed. Investigators had evidence—the mask, sperm, hairs, teeth marks, and witnesses but Bundy was not known in the state of Florida. 'Confronted by a power that is law, the subject who is constituted as subject—who is "subjected"—is he who obeys. To the formal homogeneity of power in these various instances corresponds the general form of submission in the one who is constrained by it— whether the individual in question is the subject opposite the monarch, the citizen opposite the state, the child opposite the parent, the disciple opposite the master. A legislative power on one side, and an obedient subject on the other.'[199]

Bundy transgressed all law. Subjected by state, society, family, and lover, he stole, lied, denied, and raped. He who obeys—son, student, assistant—became he who should be obeyed—dominant partner, lawyer, police officer. His victims became the subjects opposite the monarch, the disciples opposite the master; in his trials, Bundy became the citizen opposite the state but with the full power of the law—he became both in his killings and in the trials of his killings both legislative power and obedient subject.

Having failed to lure 14-year-old Leslie Parmenter into a van he had stolen from FSU, Bundy travelled south to Lake City where he abducted Kimberly Leach on the 9th of February. Two months later, police discovered her decomposed body in a

Suwannee County state park. Bundy later confessed to kidnap, murder, and rape of the young girl. A Pensecola police officer arrested Bundy for driving a stolen orange VW on the 15th of February. Subsequent searches and investigation found fibres, semen, and blood linking Bundy with the Florida killings.

Bundy once again defended himself but the evidence—including eyewitnesses, dental identification, and forensic evidence—swayed the jury. They found him guilty of two accounts of murder and two of assault and battery. On the 30th of July, he received two life sentences for the assaults and two deaths sentences for the homicides. On the 7th of January, Bundy stood trial for the killing of Kimberly Leach. As the plea was guilty by reason of insanity, Bundy did not represent himself but—in front of the judge, jury, prosecutors and his own defence team—put on a mask (one of the many real and psychological ones he would wear) of insanity, acting agitated, losing his temper, and shouting at witnesses. As in the sorority house trial, forensic evidence and eyewitnesses proved too much for the defence and, on the 9th of February, Bundy received another death sentence.

During the sorority house trials, Bundy's estranged mother pleaded for her son's life. While the Leach court was in session, Bundy asked Carole Ann Boone (a witness for the defence) to marry him and—because she accepted within a court of law—they were officially married. Bundy had asked his mother to officially pledge that he was her son, and asked his long-term partner to be his wife despite fears of rejection.

After a number of appeal requests and stays of execution, Bundy spent his time awaiting death by electric chair on Raiford Penitentiary's Death Row. While there, he confessed to writers Stephen G. Michaud and Hugh Aynesworth, FBI Special Agent William Hagmaier, and attorney Polly Nelson. In a series of meetings, Bundy assisted Detective Bob Keppel in his hunt for the 'Green River Killer.' He confessed to Keppel the seriousness of his crimes, going into details about locations, sequence of events, and his feelings at the time of the crimes. Bundy revealed for the first time that he had sex with the bodies of his victims, that his extreme perversion had become compulsive. 'My pain is constant and sharp and I do not hope for a better world for anyone. In fact, I want my pain to be inflicted on others. I want no one to escape. But even after admitting this—and I have countless times, in just about every act I've committed—and coming face-to-face with these truths, there is no catharsis. I gain no deeper knowledge about myself, no new understanding can be extracted from my telling. There has been no reason for me to tell you any of this. This confession has meant nothing.'[200]

Bundy used blunt-force trauma and strangulation to incapacitate and murder his victims. He raped and sodomized them pre-, peri-, and post-mortem. He mutilated them, dismembered them, decapitated them, and returned to their bodies to rape and sodomize them again. In his early crimes, he completely eradicated any signs of himself—the double non-existence—police found no fingerprints or blood. In his break-in murders, the victims were killed before they could cry out, he raped them in silence, sodomized their bodies in the night, inserted things into their vaginas—'Lacanian symbolic Law prohibiting direct access to the Thing ... in which the central place of Power is also empty ... the Thing is prohibited, its place is empty, and the same danger lurks: that of direct contact with the Thing (libidinal incest, political totalitarianism)...'[201] Each of Bundy's actions involved ritual: the mask, the cast, the uniform, the stripping of the bodies, the return to the corpse to re-enact the transgressive contact with the Thing, to relive his always repressed double libidinal incest with his sister/ mother. As well as heads, he took photographs of the bodies as trophies. Psychiatrists determined variously that Bundy suffered from bipolar disorder, psychoses, multiple personality disorder. Bundy admitted that he found it impossible to feel guilt or remorse and he blamed the killings on many other factors, distancing himself from responsibility for the events. He blamed the machinery of power—his father/ grandfather, his unknown father, his mother, police, courts, the media. He blamed society for his necrophiliac murders and, at 7am on January the 24th, society—in the form of police, doctors, lawyers, journalists and cheering crowds inside and outside the prison walls—witnessed or heard reports of his death by electrocution. 'Hence capital punishment could not be maintained except by invoking less the enormity of the crime itself than the monstrosity of the criminal, his incorrigibility, and the safeguard of society. One had the right to kill those who represented a kind of biological danger to others.'[202]

Sergeant François Bertrand as classic necrophile received a one-year prison sentence then disappeared from history. 120 years later, Ted Bundy, as homicidal necrophile, fried in an electric chair. Both men driven to release their sexual and violent urges in the presence of a corpse. 'In fact some, if they noticed my absence, might feel an odd, indefinable sense of relief. This is true: the world is better off with some people gone. Our lives are not all interconnected. That theory is crock. Some people truly do not need to be here.'[203]

10

NecroBanality

'The trouble with Eichmann was precisely that so many were like him, and that the many were neither perverted nor sadistic, that they were, and still are, terribly and terrifyingly normal. From the viewpoint of our legal institutions and of our moral standards of judgment, this normality was much more terrifying than all the atrocities put together, for it implied—as had been said at Nuremberg over and over again by the defendants and their counsels—that this new type of criminal, who is in actual fact *hostis generis humani*, commits his crimes under circumstances that make it well-nigh impossible for him to know or to feel that he is doing wrong.'[204]

On the 12th of June 1978, a New York court sentenced 25-year-old David Berkowitz, known to the media as Son of Sam, to a maximum 365 years for six murders and seven attempted murders in NYC between the summers of 1976 and 1977. Six days before the announcement, 18-year-old Jeffrey Dahmer gave a ride to Steven Hicks hitchhiking near Bath, Ohio. Dahmer took him back to his father's house where the two drank beer and had sex. When the 19-year-old Hicks attempted leave, Dahmer struck him with a 10lb weight and then crushed his throat with the barbell. He had sex with the body, dismembered it, put it in plastic bags under the house's crawl space, then stripped it of flesh, broke the bones down into smaller pieces, and then buried them in the woods near the house alongside the dead animals he had dissected over the years. Thirteen years later, he would confess that he murdered because 'the guy wanted to leave and I didn't want him to.' Hannah Arendt again, 'The sad truth is that most evil is done by people who never make up their minds to be good or evil.'[205]

On the 20th of December 1978, police visited the house of John Wayne Gacy in Newport Park, Illinois, not far from Chicago O'Hare International Airport. The police had had Gacy under surveillance for suspected involvement in a number of murders after finding suspicious evidence in his house. On this occasion, the officers detected the aroma of decomposing flesh. Two days later, after excavating under Gacy's crawl space, officers found human bones and arrested him for murder. Gacy quickly confessed to 30 murders of young men and boys between 1972 and 1978. Offering jobs or money for sex, Gacy would incapacitate the young men and strangle them while having sex with them and/ or raping them. Eight days after Gacy's arrest, 33-year-old Dennis Nilsen, murdered Stephen Dean Holmes whom he had met during a binge-drinking session in the Cricklewood Arms, London. Nilsen took the boy home where they drank more alcohol and spent the night together. The next morning, Nilsen strangled the 14-year-old boy with a tie and then plunged his head into a bucket of water to drown him. Nilsen confessed to police in 2006, after identifying a photograph of Stephen Holmes, that he had killed because he was scared the boy would leave. Nilsen placed the body under the floorboards of his flat, taking it out from time to time to have sex with it, before burying the decomposed body in the back garden of the house on Melrose Avenue, Cricklewood.

Although born 15 years and 4,000 miles apart, the lives and crimes of two homosexual necrophiles had many similarities and connections and shared many traits with the lives of Gein, Christie, Bundy, and West. Confusingly, Aggrawal classifies Dahmer as a class iXf necrophile—the same classification as Bundy—in that he tortured and had sex while his victims were living, killed them, mutilated them, and had sex with the dead bodies. However, Dahmer and Nilsen's victims were men, their crimes were homosexual in nature, they had oral and anal sex with the bodies. This would surely put Dahmer and Nilsen into

Aggrawal's category of Type III homosexual necrophiles who have sex with both living and dead males, but the author claims there are no reported cases despite including a case study of Dahmer and surely being aware of Nilsen's crimes.

Ritual, the use and abuse of alcohol, depression and loneliness pervaded the lives of these two men who shared a parallax view of love, sex, and abandonment. 'One leaves the village or the city, only to return. The jumps may be regulated not only by presignifying rituals but also by a whole imperial bureaucracy passing judgment on their legitimacy. The jumps are not made at random, they are not without rules. Not only are they regulated, but some are prohibited: Do not overstep the outermost circle, do not approach the innermost circle ... There is a distinction between circles because, although all signs refer to each other only to the extent that they are deterritorialized, oriented toward the same center of signifiance, distributed throughout an amorphous continuum, they have different speeds of deterritorialization attesting to a place of origin (temple, palace, house, street, village, bush, etc.), and they have differential relations maintaining the distinction between circles or constituting thresholds in the atmosphere of the continuum (private and public, family incident and social disorder). Moreover, the distribution of these thresholds and circles changes according to the case. Deception is fundamental to the system. Jumping from circle to circle, always moving the scene, playing it out somewhere else: such is the hysteric operation of the deceiver as subject, answering to the paranoid operation of the despot installed in his center of signifiance.'[206] And, 'For even violence can be submitted to a marginal ritual treatment, that is, to an evaluation of the "last violence" insofar as it impregnates the entire series of blows (beyond which another regime of violence would begin). We previously defined primitive societies by the existence of anticipation-prevention mechanisms. Now we can see more clearly how these mechanisms are constituted and distributed: it is the evaluation of the last as limit that constitutes an anticipation and simultaneously wards off the last as threshold or ultimate (a new assemblage).'[207]

It is not certain that Dahmer and Nilsen were aware of the crimes and arrests of Berkowitiz and Gacy, but both men were of above-average intelligence and both had access to news stories, so it is not beyond the stretch of the imagination that these notorious serial killers had some influence on Dahmer and Nilsen's first lust murders.

Both men grew up in rural landscapes—Dahmer in Ohio, USA, Nilsen in Fraserburgh, Scotland. Both had spells in the army—the imperial bureaucracy—where they were both initially successful (Dahmer for two years, Nilsen for eleven) and then both men gravitated to the city, Dahmer becoming a mixer in a chocolate factory in Milwaukee, Nilsen—extending his stint in imperial bureaucracy—a Metropolitan police officer and then a civil servant in a job centre in Kentish Town, London. Both left the village, the rural, to enter the city, only to return within the confines of their small flats, their small apartments, to the confines of the village, the dead animals found on solitary walks became the lone men in bars and pubs. Violence and lust regulated by the availability or unavailability of male partners. Dahmer joined the army; Nilsen did, too. They were legitimately learning how to kill—the rituals of violence. The move to the city intensified and accelerated their drive to necrophilia.

Both Dahmer and Nilsen's parents divorced (family incident), both used alcohol as a means of overcoming prohibition; joining the army (social disorder) regulated their desires, gave them rules within rules to countermand their lust. Doing so brought them within a circle within a circle, circumscribed their actions and yet deterritorialized them from the outside, gave them a conscience within a determined ethical and moral machine because they had no conscience without that machine, as they were not organs of the social machine. They had no centres of significance—fixed morals, fixed meanings—but they existed in a continual amorphous realm of *signifiance*, transgressive meaning, beyond the social, a realm of decomposing signs and bodies.

Dahmer and Nilsen met their victims in bars or pubs, offered them money, food, or shelter to lure the men back to their apartments. Deception became a fundamental part of their ritual, their means of bringing their bodies into the thresholds of their apartments, the inner circle of their lusts, the topography of control and release. They were the despot of their 'center of signifiance,' the men becoming victims in the paranoid operations of Jeff and Dennis. Both Dahmer and Nilsen incapacitated their victims— Dahmer attempted to make zombies of the men by drilling holes in their skulls and using a needle to inject boiling water or hydrochloric acid; Nilsen enjoyed strangling them while they were eating a meal he had prepared—this 'last violence' an attempt to stop the men leaving, only for the post-mortem sex to not be enough, the bodies merely bodies, not companions, and therefore yet another regime of violence and sex would have to begin. The last would always be the limit—incapacitation through drugs, alcohol, or violence, sex, death, sex again— alcohol for Dahmer and Nilsen the trigger to explode any preventive morals, the suppression of any conscience, and the stimulator of anticipation. The men, the victims, the zombies, the bodies becoming new assemblages of desire, passive vessels of infiltration and defilement, then becoming meat to be consumed or obliterated.

Writing about Andy Warhol's work, Fredric Jameson states, '...it is as though the external and coloured surface of things— debased and contaminated in advance by their assimilation to glossy advertising images—has been stripped away to reveal the deathly black-and-white substratum of the photographic negative which subtends them. Although this kind of death of the world of appearance becomes thematized in certain of Warhol's pieces—most notably, the traffic accidents or the electric chair series—this is not, I think, a matter of content any longer but of some fundamental mutation both in the object world itself—now become a set of texts or simulacra – and in the disposition of the subject.'[208]

Dahmer and Nilsen's victims were simulacra, fundamental mut(il)ations of would-be perfect partners—passive, silent, compliant. Dahmer/ Nilsen were addicted to glossy hardcore pornography—Dahmer's video collection included porno-graphic titles: *Cocktales*, *Tall Dark and Handsome*, *Rock Hard*, *Hard Men II*, *Peep Show*, and *Tropical Heat Wave*; Nilsen petitioned the courts while imprisoned to allow him to receive copies of the hardcore gay porn magazine Vulcan. Both men used the images of gay sex to lure men back to their apartments, to watch a simulation of their desires. Dahmer took photographs of his victims' dead bodies, reducing them to movie stills (stiffs), repre-sentations of the photographs they masturbated over as he then masturbated over the corpses. Death and bodies became a thematized and ritualized part of Dahmer/ Nilsen's eroticism, their death in the world, mut(il)ating the victims into an appearance of a submissive lover, a simulacra, an other. The bodies became collages of Jeff and Denis's desires and fantasies, mixed body parts, multimedia, the flip side of Richard Hamilton's *Just what is it that makes today's homes so different, so appealing?*

Jameson singles out Warhol's automobile accidents and instruments of capital punishment as representations of the death of the world of appearance, and it is worth noting that Berkowitz used a Ballardian necro-erotic stylized automobile accident—he targeted young couples in cars to murder—as his modus operandi. 'In our wounds we celebrated the re-birth of the traffic slain dead, the deaths and injuries of those we had seen dying by the roadside and the imaginary wounds and postures of the millions yet to die.'[209] Gacy used a killing device to execute his victims and ultimately died by lethal injection.

Gacy also painted portraits and erotica that are sub-Warholean, even primitive. To Warhol and to Dahmer/ Nilsen, the object aestheticized or eroticized is fundamentally dead, it has no being apart from its image, the image of and over which one masturbates, replacing the object with its copy, with its subject (as passive 'thing'), the body becoming rejectamenta, the person no longer, just something to be used and then to be disposed of.

For Dahmer/ Nilsen, living human beings were simulacra, they were copies of copies of copies of objects of desire to be mut(il)ated into yet more copies until the subjects (torn, tattered, erased, decomposed) had to be disposed of, annihilated, or turned into things. Nilsen—after keeping the bodies for a few days or weeks—cut them up and flushed them down the toilet. Dahmer kept them for weeks, sometimes dismembering them, keeping body parts—heads, hands, torsos, organs, genitalia—in a refrigerator, freezer, filing cabinet, kettle. One photograph of the head and hands of an Afro-American man resembles the dearticulated, deterritorialized masturbatory devices found in sex shops—a copy of a copy of a copy, so attenuated that it becomes its own phenomena, takes on a 'death' of its own. Jameson writing about the hyperrealist lifecasts of artist Duane Hanson writes: 'The ultimate contemporary fetishization of the human body, however, takes a very different direction in the statues of Duane Hanson—what I have already called the simulacrum, whose peculiar function lies in what Sartre would have called the derealization of the whole surrounding world of everyday reality. Your moment of doubt and hesitation as to the breath and warmth of these polyester figures, in other words, tends to return upon the real human beings moving about you in the museum and to transform them also for the briefest instant into so many dead and flesh-coloured simulacra in their own right. The world thereby momentarily loses its depth and threatens to become a glossy skin, a stereoscopic illusion, a rush of filmic images without density. But is this now a terrifying or an exhilarating experience?'[210]

Dahmer as mixer in the chocolate factory, Nilsen as administrative officer in a job centre, both seemingly grounded in mundanity; the sweet tooth of the confectioner, the bitter tongue of the put-upon civil servant, awaiting the touch and taste of the illicit, the fetishization of the body as a collection of parts—mouth, cock, balls, anus. Dahmer/ Nilsen derealized the everyday world, their world started in the bars and pubs and finished in the apartment and flat, the refrigerator and the drains. 'I never lived in dreams of winning the pools as a solution to psychological impoverishment. I was never materialistic. My needs were the needs of a "dog" who had never been cuddled, patted, wanted, praised or rewarded. I was a viable human being forced by early circumstances into the role of "lone wolf". It was my genetic inheritance which decreed that I would possess the difference which would mark me out from "the norm". It was not these differences which spawned destructive behaviour later on in life but an utter repudiation of them by my parents, peers and a conventional repressive society then extant.'[211]

Whereas Hanson's figures have the semblance of the real—even though we encounter them in a gallery—Dahmer/ Nilsen's victims were less than real, manifested fetishizations of their pornographic fantasies. Dahmer, in taking Polaroids of his victims alive and dead in various forms of bondage and pornographic posing, his mutilation and dismemberment, attempted to return them to their pornographic existence. Nilsen's dismemberment, boiling, burning, burying, and flushing of body parts, to make them excremental, elemental, prolonged his ritual homicides, his fetishistic eroticism. A trained cook, Nilsen used his skills to break down the bodies to become 'so many dead and flesh-coloured simulacra.' Dahmer used his childhood animal experiments and amateur vivisections to do likewise. The victims of both resembling the paintings of Chaim Soutine, or the more extreme works of Francis Bacon's existential-abattoir rush of flickering human monstrosities at once exhilarating to behold and terrifying to comprehend. Deleuze writing of Bacon's portraits could be quoting Dahmer/ Nilsen, 'each time meat is presented [as pornography, as post-mortem, post-human], we touch it, smell it, eat it, weigh it.'[212] Dahmer/ Nilsen used bodies, flesh, meat as sexual sacraments. Nilsen washed his dead victims, dressed them, went to bed with them, masturbated over them, sat them in chairs so they were there to greet him when he came home. Dahmer tortured his victims, killing them during sex, photographed them pre-, peri-, and post-mortem, used their body parts as fetishes—one skull he covered in chocolate. 'But why is it an act of vital faith to choose "the scream more than the horror," the violence of sensation more than the violence of the spectacle? The invisible forces, the powers of the future—are they not already upon us, and much more insurmountable than the worst spectacle and even the worst pain? Yes, in a certain sense— every piece of meat testifies to this. But in another sense, no. When, like a wrestler, the visible body confronts the powers of the invisible, it gives them no other visibility than its own. It is within this visibility that the body actively struggles, affirming the possibility of triumphing, which was beyond its reach as long as these powers remained invisible, hidden in a spectacle that sapped our strength and diverted us. It is as if combat had now become possible. The struggle with the shadow is the only real struggle. When the visual sensation confronts the invisible force that conditions it, it releases a force that is capable of vanquishing the invisible force, or even befriending it. Life screams at death, but death is no longer this all-too-visible thing that makes us faint; it is this invisible force that life detects, flushes out, and makes visible through the scream.'[213]

This passage could be taken from Dahmer's 160-page confession, or Nilsen's 400-page autobiography—*The History of a Drowning Boy*. The heads found in Dahmer's apartment, the mouths screaming perpetually in ecstatic horror; Nilsen obsessed with the mouth, with drowning, eating, and vomit. The violence of the spectacle—pornography, exhibitionism—consumed by the violence of sensation, of sex and death, of sex with death. Dahmer/ Nilsen resorted to murder and necrophilia as a means of escaping their futures, alone and unloved, the invisible forces of bureaucracy and social stigma massed against them. To these necrophiles, the worst spectacle was their own inadequacy, their own loneliness, not the putrefying corpses, dismembered limbs, gaping abdomens, and boiling heads in saucepans. 'We are not talking about studious "evil" but human inadequacy. Men will admit to potent criminality or controlling powerful "villainy" but not "inadequacy". My crimes flowed from personal inadequacy developed over a lengthy period.'[214] 'I was completely swept along with my own compulsion. I don't know how else to put it. It didn't satisfy me completely so maybe I was thinking another one will. Maybe this one will, and the numbers started growing and growing and just got out of control, as you can see.'[215]

Every piece of meat, every torso, every skull testified to their inadequacy, their loneliness. When confronted with the visibility of the dead bodies, Dahmer/ Nilsen saw the reification of their own invisible compulsions; they saw the power, their triumph over inadequacy. By keeping the bodies to wash, mutilate, masturbate over, penetrate, they triumphed over loneliness, no longer having to fantasize alone over glossy pornography, having to hide the spectacle of their desires. To kill was to vanquish the invisible force, to release the compulsion, to befriend the corpse, the lover that will not leave. The corpse—hidden in the apartment/ flat, refrigerator/ cupboard is the invisible force of Dahmer/ Nilsen's power, their life screaming at death and their control over it. The bodies, after death, became the perfect spectacles of sensation, an organ of sex and penetration, violence and consumption. For these men, alcohol and pornography were powerful stimulants and they used both ritualistically. As did the poet Algernon Charles Swinburne who, despite making the list of candidates for the true Jack the Ripper, used Victorian pornography and the release alcohol gave him to write his masochistic and algolagniac poems but not as a stimulus to murder people.

> And blood like purple blossom at the tips
> Quivering; and pain made perfect in thy lips
> For my sake when I hurt thee; O that I
> Durst crush thee out of life with love, and die,
> Die of thy pain and my delight, and be
> Mixed with thy blood and molten into thee!
> Would I not plague thee dying overmuch?
> Would I not hurt thee perfectly? not touch
> Thy pores of sense with torture, and make bright
> Thine eyes with bloodlike tears and grievous light?
> Strike pang from pang as note is struck from note,
> Catch the sob's middle music in thy throat,
> Take thy limbs living, and new-mould with these
> A lyre of many faultless agonies?
> Feed thee with fever and famine and fine drouth,
> With perfect pangs convulse thy perfect mouth,
> Make thy life shudder in thee and burn afresh,
> And wring thy very spirit through the flesh?[216]

Despite confessions of pederasty, flagellation, and zoophilia, Swinburne's sexual fantasies—facilitated by pornography and alcohol—created bodies eroticized by and with pain, where the skin, the largest human organ, becomes deterritorialized into a region of pure sensation, of inspirational flesh, of post-conscious rapture, a body to be done with, a body subsumed into a pain/pleasure organ, not protesting, not resisting, but yielding and penetrative, bloody tears and convulsive saliva forming the necrophiliac lubricant. 'A wave with a variable amplitude flows through the body without organs; it traces zones and levels on this body according to the variations of its amplitude. When the wave encounters external forces at a particular level, a sensation appears. An organ will be determined by this encounter, but it is a provisional organ that endures as long as the passage of the wave and the action of the force, and which will be replaced in order to be posited elsewhere. "No organ is constant as regards either function or position ... sex organs sprout everywhere ... rectums open, defecate and close ... the entire organism changes color and consistency in split-second adjustments." In fact, the body without organs does not lack organs, it simply lacks the organism, that is, this particular organization of organs. The body without organs is thus defined by an indeterminate organ, whereas the organism is defined by determinate organs: "Instead of a mouth and an anus to get out of order why not have one all-purpose hole to eat and eliminate?"'²¹⁷

Dahmer/ Nilsen turned their human victims into sexual machines, the totality of the body becoming organ for their organs. Their desire for sexual company flowed through the bodies until they were unable to leave—Dahmer/ Nilsen oscillated between the need for human social contact and the desire for a passive desired machine incapable of negation, abandonment, and betrayal. The body/ organ endured as long as Dahmer/ Nilsen's organs could substantiate their passage, create waves of orgasm. As the bodies decomposed so other orifices opened, so partialities became bodies, so the bodies became synecdochal, the parts standing in for the (w)hole. The parts— the organs—no longer human, no longer the organism of Homo sapiens. The body now an indeterminate sex organ—the organism eliminated—the meat left for consumption and consummation. Dahmer/ Nilsen created ritualistic spaces within which to repeatedly kill the supreme being of their desires, 'The death of the god is produced not as metaphysical alteration (concerning the common denominator of being), but the absorption of a life avid for imperative joy in the heavy animality of death. The filthy aspects of the torn-apart body guarantee the totality of disgust where life subsides.'[218]

Between the 6th of June 1978 and the 19th of July 1991, Jeffrey Dahmer killed 17 young men aged between 14 and 31. He tortured, raped, mutilated, dismembered, and photographed most of his victims. He also performed necrophiliac acts on their bodies and cannibalised at least one of his victims. When police arrested him three days after his last killing in apartment 213 at the Oxford Apartments, 924 N. 25th Street, Milwaukee, Wisconsin, they found a human head on the bottom shelf of the refrigerator; in the freezer compartment they discovered three freezer bags containing two hearts and a severed muscle; another freezer held three more heads, a torso, and various internal organs. In a closet, along with chloroform, ether, and formaldehyde, a kettle holding two hands and male genitalia sat next to two bleached skulls. Blood covered the bed and the surrounding area. The walls and refrigerators were covered with Polaroid pictures of most of the victims—the photos showed various scenes of sex, torture, rape, death, dismemberment, and necrophilia stylized as if in extreme pornographic magazines. In cupboards and cabinets, police found five painted skulls, a skeleton, a scalp, and more male genitalia. A 57-gallon tank held three decomposing torsos. The apartment, heavily bolted and alarmed, also contained bleach, odour absorbers, and incense to hide the smell of putrefaction, plus acids and Soilex used to dissolve body parts. The tools of Dahmer's necrophiliac trade were also found—drill bits, claw hammers, hunting knife, hypodermic needles, and a handsaw.

Dennis Nilsen killed a minimum of 15 men between the 30th of December 1978 and the 26th of January 1983. He strangled them using ligatures, neckties, headphone leads, or with his bare hands, and then drowned them in buckets, sinks, and baths. He kept the bodies under floorboards, sometimes whole, sometimes dismembered, and then removed them for sex or for company. He would then dismember them and either burn the bodies or boil them and flush them down the toilet. A drain-cleaning company, called in to unblock the drains of the house at 23 Cranley Gardens, Muswell Hill, London, found what they first thought to be chicken blocking the pipes. Police questioned Nilsen who admitted his crimes and showed police the remains of two bodies hidden in a tea chest in a wardrobe.

Sentenced to 15 life terms in February 1992, Jeffrey Dahmer served his sentence in Columbia Correctional Institution in Portage, Wisconsin, became a born-again Christian, and died on 28 November 1994, beaten to death by fellow inmate Christopher Scarver. On November 4th 1983, the judge at the Old Bailey sentenced Dennis Nilsen to 25 years for six murders and two attempted murders, the Home Secretary amended this to a whole-life tariff and Nilsen remains incarcerated at HMP Full Sutton maximum-security prison working on his autobiography. 'I filled twenty notebooks my first year, thirty-one my second, nineteen my third. At this time I was as close to true remorse as I ever came. It was as if I had been in a dream that lasted eleven years, and had woken from it into a world I barely recognized. How had I ever done twenty-three killings? What had made me want to? I attempted to plumb the depths of my soul with words. I dissected my childhood and family (stultifying but hardly traumatic), my sexual history (abortive), my career in various branches of the civil service (utterly without distinction, except for the number of times I was fired for insubordination to my superiors). This done, and little learned, I began to write about the things that interested me now. I found myself with a great many descriptions of murders and sex acts performed upon dead boys. Small details began to return to me, such as the way a fingerprint would stay in the flesh of a corpse's thigh as if pressed into wax, or a cold thread of semen would sometimes leak out of a flaccid penis as I rolled it about on my tongue. The only constant thread running through my prison notebooks was a pervasive loneliness with no discernible beginning and no conceivable end. But a corpse could never walk away.'[219]

Poppy Z. Brite's 1996 novel *Exquisite Corpse*, fictionalizes a meeting between Nilsen and Dahmer. Denis Nilsen becomes the serial killer Andrew Compton who—Bundy-like—escapes prison by feigning his own death. In New Orleans, among rent boys and Voodoo fetishes he meets artist Jay Byrne (Jeffrey Dahmer). Both men are obsessed with necrophilia, cannibalism, and lust murders. 'Before, in my previous life, I'd told all my boys my real name. There had never seemed any need to do otherwise. Tonight I had been using Arthur, since none of the men who approached me were interesting. But to this man I said, "Andrew." "I'm Jay." He reached across the table to shake my hand. His grip was cool, dry, and languid. When I shook hands with a potential companion, I always slid my palm over his palm and grasped his wrist, briefly encircling it with my fingers, gauging his reaction to such an intimate, dominant touch. But now I was shocked to feel Jay doing the same to me. We both snatched our hands away and stared at one another.'[220]

11

NecroPosthuman

Born the wrong gender as far as his mother was concerned, Jerry Brudos[221] — like his contemporary Charles Manson — hated it when his mother dressed him in girl's clothes. Whereas Manson's mother neglected her child, Brudos's met any form of rebellion with psychological and physical abuse, chastising him for sexual thoughts, forcing him to clean up any nocturnal emissions, emphasizing the immorality and degradation of sex. Brudos entered his teens hating his mother, hating women, his life, and set out on the road in a necrophiliac Freudian revenge tragedy — Badlands, Weekend, The Hitcher, and Natural-Born Killers all rolled into one person.

Born in 1939, Brudos acquired a list of paraphilias — including podophilia (feet), retifism (shoes), transvestic fetishism, and voyeurism. Shoes became his main and controlling fetish and, from the age of five, he developed an obsession for black stilettos. Playing at a local dump, he found a pair of spike-heeled shoes and took them home. As he modelled them in front of the mirror, his mother walked in and screamed at him, calling him abusive names. She confiscated the shoes and threw them on the fire. This excited Brudos, the violent behaviour mixed with the forbidden. His mother forbade him to go near her shoes, this increased his desire for them and he began to steal shoes from neighbours, and even his kindergarten teacher. In his book on Fetishism and its Discontents in Post-1960 American Fiction, Christopher Kocela quotes from Lacan and uses his theory of '*das Ding*' and '*object petit a*' in an analysis of fetishes. 'It no longer surprises us when a man ejaculates at the sight of a shoe, a corset, a mackintosh; yet we would be very surprised indeed if any one of these objects could appease the hunger of an individual, no matter how extreme. ... Therefore, in speaking of imaginary satisfaction, we are thinking of something highly complex. In the Three Essays, Freud explains that instinct [drive] is not simple data but is rather composed of diverse elements which are dissociated in cases of perversion.'[222]

Brudos associated shoes with the forbidden, the forbidden became his focus of revenge, the ultimate forbidden thing—the death of his mother, the ejaculation into and over the withdrawn, confiscated, and destroyed shoes—the withheld, forbidden, and hidden vagina. They are cut off from reality, Brudos using them (or misusing them—they are now products of inutility) as representations of the hymen, marriage, and mother. Kraft-Ebbing writes, 'By a transference through association of ideas, gloves or shoes obtain the significance of a fetich [sic]. Max Dessoir ... points out that among the customs of the middle ages drinking from the shoe of a beautiful woman (still to be found in Poland) played a remarkable part in gallantry and homage. The shoe also plays an important role in the legend of Aschenbrödel (Cinderella).'[223]

However, the Prince did not become a murderous necrophile. A closer look at shoe fetishism provides an insight to Brudos's escalating paraphilia and murderous desires.

'By fetichists ... I understand individuals whose sexual interest is concentrated exclusively on certain parts of the female body, or on certain portions of female attire. One of the most frequent forms of this fetishism is that in which the female foot or shoe is the fetich, and becomes the exclusive object of sexual feeling and desire. It is highly probable, and shown by a correct classification of the observed cases, that the majority and perhaps all of the cases of shoe fetishism, rest upon a basis of more or less conscious masochistic desire for self-humiliation.'[224]

In Luis Buñuel's 1955 Ensayo de un Crimen (The Criminal Life of Archibaldo de la Cruz), young Archibaldo de la Cruz is chastised by his governess for wearing her black high-heel shoes, he is forced to take them off. Later, he witnesses her death, shot by a stray bullet during the Mexican Revolution. He stands over the woman's body and is eroticized by the sight of blood, stockings, long legs, and black high-heel shoes. Susana Medina's film, *Buñuel's Philosophical Toys* examines Buñuel's use of fetish images in his films—crucifixes, wedding dresses, music boxes heads of hair; but, mostly, shoes and feet, mostly black high heels. 'High heels with their emphasis on gravity and minimal contact with the earth. High heels are over-determined objects in terms of thought translated into matter.'[225] In her novel of the same name, Medina analyses what it is to be a pervert, a shoe-fetishist, and in what varying degrees can that turn one—as in the case of Buñuel's Archibaldo de la Cruz—into a murderer.

'What was a pervert? What was a fetishist? Was it a question of degree? Was his life dominated by boots, by shoes, underwear or whatever? I myself had struggled to be different, had done everything possible to be different, but this struggle for authen-ticity was probably only a pose. Or worse, not a personal decision but something imposed from without.'[226]

Brudos is a classic Freudian example of castration and Oedipus complex—the shoes replacing his mother's vagina, replacing his own penis in one hermaphroditic object. Excising his victims' breasts took from them their femininity in revenge for the confiscation of the shoes, the initial castration. Brudos acquired shoes and started a collection that he hid from his mother. He also began to steal and buy women's underwear, which he also hid. This tri-fetish of shoes, underwear, and hidden—the eternal return of the forbidden—increased his sexual arousal when in the presence of his fetish objects that were at once forbidden, erotic, and comforting.

After suffering years of humiliation by his mother, at the age of 17, not long after the release of Buñuel's *The Criminal Life of Archibaldo de la Cruz*, Brudos enacted his first sexual revenge. His fetishism, and the fantasies accrued around it, escalated dangerously. He excavated part of a local hill in which to keep women as sex slaves. To populate it, he kidnapped a young woman, pulled a knife on her and forced her to strip. Threatening her with mutilation and rape, he took photographs of her naked body and beat her.

Police arrested him and courts sentenced Brudos to nine months in Oregon State Hospital's psychiatric ward where doctors diagnosed him as borderline schizophrenic. Like Christie and West, Brudos had an obsession with the positioning of dead women's bodies, fitting them into small spaces. Christie's cupboards, West's tiny graves—for Brudos it was freezers, the frozen bodies rearranged in pornographic tableau; a murderous precursor of the artist Marc Quinn's frozen head 'Self' and his sculptures of Kate Moss, Pamela Anderson, and Allanah Starr. Although Foucault questions the nineteenth-century focalization of sex as a casual power, stating, 'the most discrete event in one's sexual behaviour—whether an accident or a deviation, a deficit or an excess—was deemed capable of entailing the most varied consequences throughout one's existence,'[227] in Brudos's case, the events of his childhood seem to have had a major influence on his desires for revenge, death, and necrophilia. By the age of 17, Brudos was stealing underwear and shoes, his attempts at developing normal male-female relationships foundering under the severe restrictions set by his mother or because of his strange behaviour.

Like Christie and Bundy, Brudos tried to live a normal life, at least socially. After an unsuccessful spell in the military (discharged for delusional tendencies), Brudos became an electrician and, in 1961, married a 17-year-old woman variously called by biographers Ralphene, Darcie, or Susan (police arrested her as an accomplice but the court acquitted her of any wrong doing. She divorced Brudos in 1970 and moved to a secret location under an assumed name). Outwardly, their life was no different to any other young couple. But soon Brudos forced his wife to parade around the house in bra and panties and increased his voyeuristic obsession by taking photographs of her naked, wearing high-heel shoes while cleaning and cooking. His fetishism, 'this obscene underground, the unconscious terrain of habits, [was] what [was] really difficult to change,'[228] and rather than change it, he amplified it. He forbade his wife to enter the loft or his garage workshop. After their two children were born, their sex life stopped. This may have been a result of Brudos's transvestism, underwear theft, and/or collection of nude photography.

Seven years into his marriage, Brudos killed 19-year-old college student Linda Slawson. An opportunistic murder, Brudos asked the door-to-door encyclopaedia saleswoman into his garage in Salem, Oregon, to talk about a purchase, then beat her with a piece of wood and strangled her to death. Excited by this reification of his erotic fantasies, he gave his mother, wife and two children money to go treat themselves to burgers. Once they had left, he returned to the garage bringing with him his extensive collection of underwear and shoes. He stripped the body, added her red panties to his collection, and then dressed her in lingerie. He cut off her left foot with a hacksaw, put it into a stiletto-heel shoe, and stashed it in the freezer. The rest of the body, he weighted down with an engine block and—like Bundy had done with some of his victims—dumped it in a nearby river never to be discovered. Police discovered the woman's abandoned car but follow-up enquiries found nothing suspicious. Brudos spent weeks putting the amputated foot into shoes from his collection, taking photographs of it and masturbating over it. Once it had decomposed, he threw it into the river.

Within a year, his manic desire had returned and, on the 26th of November 1968, another opportunity presented itself for him to murder. 23-year-old Jan Whitney's car had broken down on freeway 1-5 near Albany, Oregon, and Brudos stopped and asked if she needed a lift. He drove to his garage on the pretence that he could fix her car. There, he incapacitated her, hung her up, and strangled her to death. He took the body down and spent the rest of the day dressing it in costumes. He took photographs and sexually abused the body, repeatedly raping it vaginally and anally. He then placed the body on a hook and pulley hanging from the ceiling and left it there over the Thanksgiving holidays. While away, an accident occurred and police investigated a car crash that damaged the garage. They did not ask to look inside but Brudos became paranoid. In a similar manner to Bundy's crimes, Brudos cut off one of Whitney's breasts, photographed the body, and dumped it in the Williamette River. Like Gein, he used the breast as a 'thing'—a paperweight solidified with epoxy resin. The trophies of Christie (pubic hair), Gein (body parts), Bundy (heads), West (bones), and Brudos are Lacanian objects of drive, stimulating and enacting desires; *Objet petit a*, partial objects defining the drives. But they are also objects of anxiety and libido, the desire to control and regain the whole body and the desire for the metonymic part of it. Brudos's fetishes were erotic and ritualistic, they were also commodities.

His desires increasing and accelerating, Brudos killed his third victim four months after he murdered Jan Whitney. Karen Sprinker had been visiting the Meier & Frank department store where she was supposed to have lunch with her mother. Walking to her car in the parking lot, Brudos—dressed as a woman—abducted her at gunpoint on the 27th of March 1969. He drove her back to his garage, raped her, made her dress up (he didn't like the shoes she was wearing) and pose for photographs, took her underwear for his fetish trophies, and then hung her from the ceiling before garrotting her. After repeatedly raping the corpse, he cut off the breasts. 'Her breasts had been chopped off and they look blue and deflated, the nipples a disconcerting shade of brown. Surrounded by dried black blood, they lie, rather delicately on a china plate I bought at Pottery Barn on top of the Wurlitzer jukebox in the corner, though I don't remember doing this.'229

Partial objects of commodification, the reduction to things, to objects of possession to objects of obsession to objects of desire. After stuffing a bra from his lingerie stash with wadded paper towels and covering her mutilated chest with it, Brudos weighted the body, redressed it, and threw it in the Long Tom River. Police discovered it two months later, after they had discovered the corpse of Brudos's next victim.

Desire escalated and accelerated, Brudos killed again four weeks later. Like Christie before him and Bundy later, Brudos pretended to be a police officer and arrested 23-year-old Linda Salee for shoplifting in a shopping mall. He drove her to his garage, bound her, took a break to eat lunch, returned and raped her while strangling her to death with surgical thread. Brudos kept the body in his garage for a few days, raping it, trying to take moulds of Salee's breasts, he later hung the corpse from the ceiling and, using needles and jump wires, shot electricity through it to watch the corpse dance. Again, he weighted the body with a transmission box, bound it with nylon rope and dumped it in the Long Tom River where an angler discovered it two weeks later.

Police caught Brudos on the 25th of May 1969 setting a trap for him after a woman reported that he had acted strange on a date, that he was stalking students at a local college and had attempted to abduct a teenage girl. When the police arrested him, they found that he was wearing women's panties. When police forensic officers searched Brudos's home, they discovered the hook-and-pulley system, nylon cords, leather straps, a mould of the amputated breast, women's shoes, underwear, and photographs of Brudos dressed in women's clothing and of his victims in various stages of dress, torture, and decomposition—in most of the photographs, the heads are not visible or are hooded. One shot showed a woman's body hanging from the ceiling, dressed in black lace lingerie, the point of view as from the woman's vagina shown in a mirror between her feet, Brudos staring obliviously at the reflected dead body.

If Brudos was part Archibaldo de la Cruz, he was also part Norman Bates from Hitchcock's *Psycho*—a cross-dressing, mother-obsessed, women hater. Despite his defence arguing that he was insane, Brudos pleaded guilty to the three murders (Linda Slawson's body was never found) and the court sentenced him to three consecutive life sentences. Despite numerous appeals and parole hearings, he remained incarcerated and became the longest-serving prisoner in the US. He died in Oregon State Penitentiary on 29 March 2006.

Like Christie, Brudos developed fetishes and the desire to kill and rape women as revenge attacks on his mother. Like Bundy, he would rape the victims pre-, peri- and post-mortem. Like Bundy and West, he would then mutilate the corpses and take trophies. Like Gein, he would turn the body parts into household objects. Brudos's obsessive desires ranged from harmless shoe fetishism to anal necrophilia. His lust for murder, body parts, shoes, and mutilation escalated. A number of women had escaped Brudos's attempts to abduct them. There may have been more undetected bodies of young white females who happened to go missing. Brudos, arrogant and with no conscience or remorse, admitted only what he had to. During psychiatric tests, Brudos confessed that—like Archibaldo de la Cruz and his fetish mannequin, like Hans Bellmer's Die Puppe—he wanted a human doll he could dress, pose, photograph, and have sex with. Like Bertrand, Christie, West, and Gein, Brudos claimed to have had blackouts and to be detached from reality while committing his crimes, later blaming his actions on his mother.

In Buñuel's *The Criminal Life of Archibaldo de la Cruz*, as Archibaldo drags the mannequin to his workshop to burn it, to rid himself of at least one of his fetishes, a leg and shoe fall off signifying not only Archibaldo's separation from reality but his initial separation from his mother—the instigation of his multiple fetishes. Brudos's amputation of feet, breasts, and other body parts actualized in his mind his mother's separation and her confiscation of the black high-heel shoes—in Brudos's mind, the same event. He desired to incapacitate bodies, freeze them, and arrange them in erotic poses as forbidden and pliable mother substitutes. As Archibaldo burns the mannequin in a furnace, it appears to become alive and dance—in its death it has become the real object of desire. Similarly, Brudos electrified the corpse of Linda Salle to watch it dance.

Hans Bellmer's dolls prefigured both Buñuel's mannequin and Brudos's victims. In an essay on Bataille and Bellmer, Elliott Vanskike observes, 'The Doll that Bellmer constructed in the early 1930s was a female mannequin, outfitted with a wig and articulated by means of ball joints so that the arms and legs could be manipulated. Bellmer varied the settings for the photographs of his Doll—beds, staircases, the forest. And he varied the arrangement of the mannequin. But whether it was clothed in a chemise and child's patent leather shoes, or assembled with arms or legs missing or grotesquely rearranged, the Doll was always posed to suggest a certain degraded innocence, an unsettling juxtaposition of childish naïveté and adult depravity.'[230]

Like Brudos's victim in his photographs, like Bundy's bodies, many of Bellmer's dolls had no heads. The dolls and posed bodies—in West's case, bodies taped until they could not move—were manipulated to cater for Bellmer/ Bundy/ Bataille/ Brudos's desires. How murderers and artists meet is apparent here—in the disturbed gaze—in which they: 'explore the limits and potential of desire, the power of desire not just to form the desired object, but to unmake the maker. Confronted by the Doll, the viewer sees the stable dialectic between self and other collapse. To use Bataille's formulation of this confrontation, "we are faced with the paradox of an object which implies the abolition of all objects, of an erotic object."'[231]

12

NecroCalculus

From Karen Greenlee to Jeffery Dahmer by way of Sergeant Bertrand, the sliding scale of necrophiliac desire is obvious. Greenlee's available and opportunistic macabre frottage is separated by moral leaps and bounds from the disinternement evisceration, masturbation and sexual penetration perpetrated by Sergeant Bertrand, which is again far from approaching in immoral standards the sadistic murder and rape of young men by Jeffrey Dahmer. As observers of these acts, we have to ask ourselves: why would and how could these people have sex—in whatever fashion—with dead bodies? Are they immoral? Are they insane? Are they evil? Is it a matter of sexual desire? Is it an uncontrollable paraphilia? Or is it that necrophiles do not experience disgust as much as or in the same way as other people? And if so, if it is a matter of sexual proclivity mixed with anosmia, should we deny them their rights however non-ethical they are? 'Refusing the same ethical rights to those outside our community as those inside it is something that does not come naturally to a human being. It is a violation of our spontaneous ethical proclivity. It involves brutal repression and self-denial.'[232]

Carl von Cosel had sex with the dead body of Maria Elena Milagro de Hoyos because he was in love with her dead and/ or alive. Necrophilia for von Cosel was a furtherance of his obsessive desire for the 22-year-old woman. For Ted Bundy, necrophilia was just another means of degrading the women he attacked, another way to exercise his power. So is necrophilia a form of love or a form of rape? Whom does it harm? In Karen Greenlee's case, we could argue that no(body) was harmed, relatives may have been perturbed and newspapers shocked but there was no injury to the bodies, no psychological torture for the 'victims'. In the case of Sergeant Bertrand, again, no(body) experienced pain—beside Bertrand—even if the bodies were mutilated; the people most shocked by the acts appeared to be the gravediggers and the doctors who interviewed the sergeant. But once we move on to Dahmer and Bundy, our moral outrage becomes more pronounced, these men killed for pleasure, they killed because they enjoyed physical and psychological violence, rape and necrophilia. '"Violence," here, is not aggression as such, but its excess, which disturbs the normal run of things by desiring always more and more.'[233] For Greenlee, corpses were akin to vibrators. For Bertrand, dead bodies were like Fleshlights within which he could fulfil his necro fantasies. For Dahmer and Bundy, their victims were human beings that they reduced to nothing through torture, rape and murder. This is where our immoral calculus may help us.

As William T. Vollmann states, 'Death is ordinary',[234] it happens to everybody, yet necrophilia happens to very, very few. Dead bodies are covered in faeces, in urine, they stink of rotten flesh, they exude noxious gases. Is having sex with a dead body immoral or is it just disgusting? Is necrophilia only immoral because of the means of acquiring the body as a vessel for sexual purposes? And if it is immoral, then are the perpetrators mad and evil perverts who will stop at nothing to satisfy their twisted sexuality? Or are they harmless opportunists with a fetish for the dead? Does necrophilia fall under the category of ethics or emotion? 'Does every ethics have to rely on fetishist disavowal? Is even the most universal ethics not obliged to draw a line and ignore some sort of suffering?'[235] Is it a question of moral negligence, moral indifference, moral weakness or moral perversity? Is it a form of preferential wickedness? Is it amoral rather than immoral?[236] And if we decide that it is immoral, then is it evil? In order to study these labels in regards to necrophilia, the case of various contemporary necrophiles will be taken into consideration.

Born in 1968, Graham Coutts had had violent sexual fantasies about women from his early teens and became an asphyxiophiliac, using self-asphyxiation to heighten and lengthen his orgasms. Coutts enjoyed what he termed 'breath control sex' and used this both passively and actively with his partners. Passive asphyxiophilia (the asphyxiation of a partner in order to render them unconscious) could be considered a training method for certain forms of necrophilia. The unconscious body becomes a sexual plaything for the active partner. Yet active asphyxiophilia in which one strangles oneself in order to heighten orgasm is anti-necrophilia in that it is attempted suicide for sexual purposes.

Coutts was a sexual experimenter, a man who enjoyed extreme pornography—he had bought DVDs such as *Psycho Sisters* and *Murder x2* and paid over £100 in membership fees to pseudo-snuff and sadist websites Club Dead, Brutal Love and Twistedfiles.com, he fantasized about rape but was also a man who had a steady job and long-term girlfriend. In March 2003, he was in the company of Jane Longhurst, a friend of his girlfriend at his home in Brighton, England. Coutts told the court at his trial that he and Jane had had consensual sex, that he had wrapped a pair of tights around her neck and that her subsequent death had been an accident while performing asphyxiophilia. Erotic obsession had turned to murder. Coutts, like Christie, had pre- and peri-mortem sex with the body; whether or not he had intended to kill Jane Longhurst, after the strangulation, he had the 'opportunity' to act out one of his fantasies, to have sex with a dead woman, going against Terry Eagleton's statement about Freud that 'there is a sense in which we find death extraordinarily gratifying.'[237] However, Coutts had to overcome something that we would all feel, not a sense of the immorality of the act but that primal emotion of disgust. Coutts had kept the body for a month in various locations, until he placed her decomposing body in a storage unit, visiting the body on a number of occasions during that period. But Coutts claimed in court, 'There's nothing sexual about a dead body, nothing. And the smell was getting worse and worse and worse. There's nothing remotely sexual about that.' Did Coutts overcome his feelings of disgust to rape the dead body of Jane Longhurst?

Disgust—be it pathogenic, sexual or moral—must be overcome in order to perform a necrophiliac act. Pathogenic disgust has its basis in evolutionary human morality protecting us against disease, decay, dead bodies, most people have a primary emotional response to the sight of urine, faeces, blood and vomit and, it must be argued, most of these bodily emissions must have been present during and after the sexual strangulation of Jane Longhurst. Sexual disgust guards us against incest and also assists in choosing a mate through body symmetry, etc. However many times Coutts may have visited the body, the sexual disgust must have increased and his attraction decreased—he eventually burned the body in local woods. If Coutts had had consensual sex with Jane Longhurst—however against the norm—and the death had been an accident, then his necrophilia was a form of post-mortem rape. However, if he had lured her to his house, raped, killed and then committed necrophilia, Coutts was beyond the barrier of any form of moral disgust. Taking all three domains together, Coutts does not appear to be overly burdened with the primal emotion of disgust. The court did not think so and in 2007, after an appeal, he was sentenced to life in prison.

What is certain is that Graham Coutts committed rape on the body of Jane Longhurst. In his 'moral calculus' Vollmann asks, 'What constitutes rape? We think we have it figured out. It is sexual knowledge without consent, or sexual knowledge of a person deemed unable to comprehendingly consent, such as a minor or a mental incompetent.'[238] This asks fundamental questions about sexual congress with a dead body? A corpse is not able to 'comprehendingly consent,' it is neither a minor nor a mental incompetent. It has no sensory stimuli, it is unable to feel pain or humiliation. For the necrophile, it is nothing more than an object of desire and a receptacle for sexual emissions. In other words, it is devalued to the point of pornography and the Coutts case led to the call in the UK government for the criminalization of extreme pornography, even though then most extreme pornography (in the case of some necrophiles) is the corpse itself.

I say, I want more for my fifty bucks than just his drooling over a dead body.

'You'da been drooling, too,' he says. 'Damn, she was a looker.'

I ask, were there valuables — watches, wallets, jewellery — left at the scene?

He says, 'Still warm, too, under the covers. Warm enough. No death agonies. Nothing.'

His big jaw goes around and around, slower now as he stares down at nothing in particular. 'If you could have any woman you wanted,' he says, 'if you could have her any way you wanted, wouldn't you do it?'

I say, what he's talking about is rape.

'Not,' he says, 'if she's dead.' And he crunches down on a potato chip in his mouth. 'If I'd been alone, alone and had a rubber...,' he says through the food. 'No way would I let the medical examiner find my DNA at the scene.'

Then he's talking about murder.

'Not if somebody else kills her,' Nash says, and looks at me. 'Or kills him. The husband had a fine-looking ass, if that's what floats your boat. No leakage. No livor mortis. No skin slippage. Nothing.'

How he can talk this way and still eat, I don't know.

He says, 'Both of them naked. A big wet spot on the mattress, right between them. Yeah, they did it. Did it and died.' Nash chews his sandwich and says, 'Seeing her there, she was better-looking than any piece of tail I've ever had.'[239]

Chuck Palahniuk's comedic use of situation and opportunity based necrophilia leads us to ask the main questions about the act and those questions are simple. How (as in terms of disgust) can a man or woman have sex with a dead body? And why (in the moral sense) would they want to? In an obsessive game of rock, paper, scissors, in the case of the necrophile, desire always wins out over disgust and morality. In the above example, the paramedic John Nash views sex with a corpse (be it a man or a woman) as neither morally wrong nor disgusting.

Whether the disgust is created by the sight of injuries caused to victims in lust murders, as in the 2005 case of Mark Dixie who stabbed Sally Anne Bowman six or seven times, bit her body and inserted concrete into his victim's mouth and vagina; or disgust is caused by the sight and smell of a dead body in a funeral home or morgue as in the case of Kenneth Douglas (2007), a morgue attendant suspected of having sex with at least 100 corpses, some of which had been involved in motor-vehicle accidents; or disgust is experienced in the sight, smell and touch of bodies taken from graves and mausoleums as in the case of the Filipino 'Tomb Raider' Randy Uro Galvez who disinterred women's bodies in order to have sex with them in 2009 and 2010; these actions should cause some form of disgust. Looking back at classic necrophilia cases, the homicidal necrophiles—Christie, Bundy and West—showed no signs of disgust for what they did; nor did the situation/ opportunistic necrophiles such as Karen Greenlee and Carl von Cosel; and—probably the most extreme cases—nor did the exhumist necrophiles Sergeant Bertrand and Ed Gein. Yet disgust has some universal indicators as Danny Kelly argues. 'An undeniable affinity holds between disgust and various sorts of organic materials. Hence at the most concrete end of the spectrum of elicitors are what Rozin and others have suggested as the best candidates to be universals: feces, vomit, blood, urine, and sexual fluids (Rozin et al. 2008; see also Angyal 1941). Equally plausible as universals are corpses and signs of organic decay, which are also some of the most potent elicitors of disgust (Haidt et al. 1994). Bodily orifices—and via contamination, things that come in contact with bodily orifices—are likewise powerful and potentially universal elicitors (Rozin et al. 1995). More generally, artificial orifices or breaches of physical bodies such as cuts, gashes, lesions, or open sores (in Rozin's terms, violations of the 'ideal body envelope') are also good candidates for disgust universals. These can trigger disgust if they occur to one's own body—in which case they probably also cause pain—or in someone else's. In this sense, disgust appears universally sensitive to the boundaries of organic bodies and in many cases is activated when those boundaries have been, or are in danger of being, breached.'[240]

All necrophiles—from Karen Greenlee to Jeffrey Dahmer transgress disgusts, they go beyond and within the 'ideal body envelope', are insensitive to the boundaries of organic bodies and their organic materials. In Cormac McCarthy's Child Of God, the necrophile Lester Ballard internalizes the disgust and makes it a cathedral of desire, a place in which 'the walls with their softlooking convolutions, slavered over as they were with wet and blood-red mud, had an organic look to them,'[241] and so incorporates his own self-disgust, his own low self-esteem by equating his victims with either animality or piety, 'like the innards of some great beast. Here in the bowels of the mountain Ballard turned his light on ledges or pallets of stone where dead people lay like saints.'[242] Ballard shows no disgust for the blood, the organs, the decaying dead. Even Peter Sutcliffe, the Yorkshire Ripper, who murdered 13 women and attempted to murder seven more from 1975 to 1980, experienced disgust at one of his murder scenes. On the 9th of October 1977, eight days after murdering Jean Jordan in Southern Cemetery, Manchester, Sutcliffe returned to the scene to look for a possibly incriminating

£5 note he had handed the prostitute before bludgeoning her across the head eleven times with a hammer. Frustrated at not being able to find the money, Sutcliffe 'stabbed her repeatedly in the breasts and chest, he snatched up a broken pane from a nearby greenhouse and opened up a wound from her right knee to her left shoulder. The stench as her stomach blew open made him vomit.'[243] But then Peter Sutcliffe considered himself 'as normal as anyone.'[244] This may be because, (v)iolence *toward* the actual pulp and mineral and water of such an organism is rare, although, like terrorism directed *at* a group *through* various unfortunate victims, violence quite frequently expresses itself by means of the destruction of the flesh. The real aim of violence is to conquer, direct, instruct, mark, warn, punish, injure, suppress, reduce, destroy or obliterate the consciousness within the body.'[245]

Peter Sutcliffe—hammer murderer, screwdriver eviscerator—responded to the eight-day-old corpse's organic material in a predictable manner, even though minutes later he attempted to behead the corpse. The object being becomes an abject being, the corpse creates disgust in us, the fear of infection, the horror of death, the void of non-being. The corpse reanimated in the vampire, the zombie, the ghoul—the living dead with their blood, their sores, their unstoppable desire to turn the 'ideal body envelope' into a corpse. In *Buffy the Vampire Slayer* and *True Blood*, the 'ideal body envelopes' inhabited by the vampires Angel and Spike (*Buffy*) and Bill and Eric (*True Blood*) are skin-deep, encasing the arrested decay and putrescence we see when the vampires are staked or beheaded. In reverse, these vampires, werewolves and zombies mock us because 'there is a funda-mental imbalance, gap, between our psychic energy, called by Freud 'libido', this endless undeadenergy which persists beyond life and death, and the poor, finite, mortal reality of our bodies.'[246] If Buffy falls for the bodies of Angel and Spike knowing that they are merely casings for disgust, how did

Sergeant Bertrand, Ed Gein and even Karen Greenlee overcome that disgust to desire a body, a decaying corpse which is '*the* emblem of the menace that, in the case of disgust, meets with such a decisive defense, as measured by its extremely potent register on the scale of unpleasureable affects. Every book about disgust is not least a book about the rotting corpse.'[247]

If, as Freud argues, 'the less repellent so called sexual perversions are the most widespread,'[248] then conversely, necrophilia is still very rare. Yet, when it is discovered, there is national and international news coverage, usually with the attendant 'ghoul' and 'vampire' sensational headlines. One such case came to the attention of the media in 2006 when Nicholas and Alexander Grunke, and Dustin Radke were arrested for the attempted disinterment and planned rape of the body of 20-year-old Laura Tennessen.[249] Nicholas Grunke became sexually attracted to Laura after seeing her photograph in a local Wisconsin newspaper. On the 27th of August, Laura had died in a motorcycle accident and a week later, Nicholas persuaded his brother and a friend to accompany him to St Charles Cemetery in Cassville in order to exhume Laura's body. The young men planned to take the corpse back to Nicholas's house in order for him to have sex with it, they'd even purchased condoms in a local Wal-Mart on their way to the cemetery. Having shovelled through the top layer of earth, the men reached the concrete vault in which Laura's coffin rested. A passerby had spotted their vehicle outside the cemetery and reported it to the police. On reaching the graveyard, the officers discovered Alexander Grunke close to the disturbed burial plot. He admitted to the attempted grave-robbing and his brother Nicolas and friend Dustin Radke were arrested soon after. Maybe the three men had been surfing the internet and discovered an article on necrophilia written in 1993 by someone called Theoderich in which he opines, 'An experienced necrophiliac is always equipped with the bare essentials: a shovel, vaseline and a box of rubbers. Why the shovel is needed should be obvious, but if the ground is hard then you might need more equipment to dig up your date. Vaseline is used to loosen the corpse up a bit. This makes it less likely for a body part to break off while you're having fun and it also prevents your mantool from becoming too irritated while screwing the dried out pussy. The BOX of condoms is used to play it safe; no necrophiliac should be without it. You never know which STDs your partner had during his/ her lifetime, and believe me, it doesn't get any better after the person dies. You can put on more than one rubber for extra protection if it is warranted, but screwing a corpse without protection is just plain stupid unless you want to be the next date for a necrophiliac.'[250]

The three men were originally sent to trial for criminal damage and theft, the judge ruling that there was no evidence of attempted sexual assault. However, in 2008, the State of Wisconsin passed the Laura Tennessen Necrophilia Law, making necrophilia (or attempted necrophilia) illegal. Although two out of the five high-court judges at the new trial argued that necrophilia was a victimless crime, Nicholas Grunke was found guilty of third-degree sexual assault. After plea-bargaining, Dustin Radke was also found guilty of third-degree sexual assault and claimed, 'Nick said numerous times over the years how he'd love to have sex with a dead body because he wouldn't want to have a woman to come home to holler at, or complain or nag at him. And he said that more than once.'[251] Making a claim that Nicholas was a classic necrophile in wanting an unresisting and partner and fearful of sexual rejection as our friend Theoderich explains, "[F]irstly, a corpse will never tell you to get off of it if you're being a bit rough and it will never complain no matter what kinky sexual practices you use it for.'[252] Alexander Grunke was also found guilty of all charges. The men were sentenced to two years in prison and Nicholas placed on a five-year supervisory psychotherapy course and added to the Wisconsin sexual offenders register. Those are the facts but what might have happened if they had reached Laura's body?

Even though Theoderich proselytizes that, '[H]opefully these vivid descriptions will encourage you to go out to your local cemetery and to join our ranks!'[253] The three young men from Wisconsin may not have thought this plan through thoroughly, after all, as Freud states, 'the impulses of sexual life are among those least effectively controlled by the higher activities of the mind.'[254] But if their scheme had worked and they had uncovered Laura Tennessen, wrapped her in the grey tarp they had thoughtfully brought with them in the van and taken her back to the garden behind the family house for Nicholas to fulfil his lust (presumable with Alexander and Dustin as voyeuristic cheerleaders), then what would they have found and how would they have coped with it? If we are 'inclined to see disgust as one of the powers which have imposed boundaries upon the sexual goal' and 'the strength of the sexual drive enjoys actively overcoming disgust,'[255] then how would these men have coped with Laura Tennessen after she had been killed in a motor-vehicle accident, undergone a post-mortem, embalming and buried for a week?

Nicholas Grunke first became attracted to Laura after reading her obituary. Could he have been sexually stimulated not only by the sight of her all-American, pretty face, white teeth and long blonde hair but also by the fact that she had died in a motor-vehicle accident in which 'the automobile, and in particular the automobile crash, provides a focus for the conceptualizing of a wide range of impulses involving the elements of psychopathology, sexuality, and self-sacrifice'[256] and 'is seen as a fertilizing rather than a destructive experience, a liberation of sexual and machine libido, mediating the sexuality of those who have died with an erotic intensity impossible in any other form.'[257] If so, Nicholas and his cohorts would have had to overcome feelings of disgust, dealing with decaying flesh, wounds, the odours of embalming and necrosis, with bodily fluids, escaping gases, maybe even insects that had begun to break down the body's tissue and organs. Was it the case that in these young men's 'sexual li[ves], abject elements, even ones that ha[d] been denied, play[ed] the determining role of agents of erotic attraction' and that 'such elements rest[ed] on the possibility—always latent—of transforming repulsion into attraction.'[258] Theoretically. In reality, would they have, like Peter Sutcliffe, vomited at the smell and sight of the body, inverting the desired-for bodily ejaculation? As the young men had bought condoms to wear during the act, then we can surmise that they had qualms about disease, about flesh on decaying flesh, about the very act of penetrating a corpse. These would-be necrophiles, these attempted-rapists, fantasized about sexual intercourse with Laura's dead body, they did not have to overcome their disgust, they imagined that that they would have a wholly compliant, non-nagging, sex toy. The embodiment and essence of a zombie. They did not act out their fantasy as had Jeffrey Dahmer, another Wisconsin citizen, 25 years previously.

This case is a reverse of the Death and the Maiden story. Laura as Persephone, but this time raised from the dead to be abducted by a triad of slacker young men and taken to their personal Hades—the Grunke's back garden. Eros and Thanatos. Rather than picking the narcissus, Persephone/ Laura was to be bedded among the flowers. As in Death and the Maiden paintings by Niklaus Manuel Deutsch, Hans Baldung Grien, Edvard Munch and Egon Schiele, the Maiden does not resist the sexual approaches of Death, she is compliant, unresisting. No fear is shown by the maiden, nor any signs of disgust. With Eros and Thanatos, desire and disgust, there is an attraction and a repellence, 'disgusting things, whether they be slugs, saliva, dead bodies or sex with dead bodies, are disgusting to us but they also *interest* us. Our intrigue with what is disgusting taps into the inherent curiosity and fascination we have with ourselves—who we are, what we are made of, and how we will die.'[259]

If, as Nietzsche writes, disgust come about through, '[t]he aesthetically insulting at work in the inner human without skin — bloody masses, muck-bowels, viscera, all those sucking, pumping monstrosities — formless or ugly or grotesque, painful for the smell to boot.' How did Bertrand, Gein and Dahmer et al deal with it? The majority of people adhere to Nietzsche's reasoning, 'Hence away with it in thought! What still does emerge excites shame ... This body, concealed by the skin as if in shame ... hence: there is disgust-exciting matter.' The body is the disgust-exciting matter yet for necrophiles it is lust-exciting matter. Nietzsche again, 'the more ignorant humans are about their organism, the lesser can they distinguish between raw meat, rot, stink, maggots.' Yet Bertrand and Gein revelled in the rot, the stink, the sexuality of raw meat. 'To the extent he is not a *Gestalt*, the human being is disgusting to himself — he does everything to not think about it.'[260] This is the embodiment and essence of the vampire — living death with all its attendant decay sheathed in a beautiful skin. Bertrand masturbated over the intestines of exhumed bodies. Gein made kitchen objects and clothing from human remains, Dahmer kept body parts in his fridge. They did not find bodies disgusting, they thought about them. How did they overcome their feelings of disgust when this strong and basic emotion is integral to structuring social and moral order?

The professions and interests of necrophiles may provide us with a clue. Sergeant Bertrand was a soldier who had seen active service in the wars and revolutions of mid-nineteenth-century France. Peter Kürten was a butcher. Fred West worked in an abattoir. Jeffrey Dahmer experimented on roadkill. Many others were employed in hospitals, mortuaries, funeral homes or cemeteries. Their relation to the human body is similar to the effects that Hans Bellmer's dolls have on the viewer, the body parts are fetishized liberating the viewer, the necrophile from ethical codes, from the habit of disgust where trauma is desire and repression surfaces. If physical disgust became sublimated by proximity to dead bodies—a perverted inversion of Freud's sublimation theory that sexual desire is transformed into social and/or cultural achievements—then certain necrophiles used this repression or overcoming of physical disgust and, in effect, expanded their sexual desire network. But how did they supplant or neglect their moral disgust. Proximity, familiarization and desensitization may also be a factor in transgressing social and personal morality.

The argument may be that '[e]very ethical act, as pure and disinterested as it may appear, is always grounded in some "pathological" motivation (the agent's own long-term interest)' and that 'desire itself (i.e., acting upon one's desire, not compromising it) can no longer be grounded in any "pathological" interest or motivation, and thus meets the criteria of the Kantian ethical act, so that "following one's desire" overlaps with "doing one's duty".'[261]

In California in February 2003, Donald Luis Cooper, pleaded guilty to the sexual abuse of Robyn Gillett, a four-year-old girl who had died from influenza. Cooper had transported her body to the San Bernardino county morgue from Victor Valley Community Hospital. As his girlfriend, Chaunee Marie Helm, stood lookout, he sexually assaulted the body but was caught on CCTV cameras. As in the case of Laura Tennessen in Wisconsin, California had no laws to criminalize necrophilia and Cooper was charged and found guilty of the felony mutilation of human remains and received a suspended two-year prison sentence. However, after breaking his parole and being charged with cruelty to animals, Cooper was sentenced to two years at the California Institution for Men in Chino in accordance to Robyn's law introduced in 2004 making necrophilia illegal in California.

Tsutomu Miyazaki abducted, raped, mutilated, killed and cannibalized four young girls between 1988 and 1989. In his mid-twenties at the time of the murders, Miyazaki was obsessed with child pornography, hentai and horror movies. He became known as the Otaku Murderer. In Japanese society, an "otaku" is an obsessive fan, usually of anime but also of lolicon, cosplay or any other obsession. In killing the four girls and sexually assaulting their bodies, Miyazaki played out his fantasies, videoing and photographing the bodies in sexually provocative poses. During the period of his crimes, he sent remnants of the bodies to the girls' parents along with mocking postcards boasting of his acts and called their houses remaining silent when the distraught parents answered the phone. After his arrest in 1989, Miyazaki claimed to have an alter ego called Rat Man. Psychiatrists clamed Miyazaki had multiple personality disorder and schizophrenia. Despite this, he was found accountable for his crimes and sentenced to death and hanged on the 17th of June 2008.

Cooper's crime was one of opportunity and proximity, Miyazaki's crimes of paedophilia and obsessive fantasy. In the four major classes of necrophilia, necrophiliac homicide-murder, in which a corpse is obtained by homicide for sexual purposes; regular [sic] necrophilia, in which already dead bodies are used for sex; necrophiliac fantasy, fantasizing about sexual intercourse with a dead body without actually committing necrophilia; and pseudonecrophilia, in which sexual activity with a corpse is only part of a wider sexuality,[262] it is apparent that necrophilia fantasy and necrophiliac homicide-murder are poles apart in any moral calculus. However, Miyazaki was both a necrophiliac fantasist and a necrophiliac-murderer. Cooper was a pseudonecrophile and a regular necrophile, opportunistically using a dead body for sex. How far outside moral norms and ethical rules are the varying types of necrophile?

A contemporary of the Marquis de Sade, Immanuel Kant argues, 'Thus it is that man lays claim to a will which does not let anything come into account if it belongs merely to his desires and inclinations, but, contrary to these, thinks of acts being possible for him, indeed necessary, which could only occur after all desires and sensory stimulation have been ignored.'[263]

Not so the necrophile. Be it a fantasist or a murderer, the necrophile obsesses on his or her desires and sensory stimulation, goes beyond any "will" to suppress their inclinations. But that is no different than the desiring drive of a paedophile, a homosexual, a heterosexual. The homicidal and the regular necrophile, however, must transgress morality and ethical standards by committing murder and rape.

Is the necrophile, in whichever guise, an anti-Kantian, a Nietzschean, rebelling against the injustices of society's ethical straitjacket? Written and published in 1887, a year before Jack the Ripper's murder spree in London, Nietzsche states in *The Genealogy of Morals*, 'Hostility, cruelty, pleasure in persecution, in assault, in change, in destruction—all that turning against the man who possesses such instincts: such is the origin of "bad conscience". The man who is forced into an oppressively narrow and regular morality, who for want of external enemies and resistance impatiently tears, persecutes, gnaws, disturbs, mistreats himself, this animal which is to be "tamed", which rubs himself raw on the bars of his cage, this deprived man consumed with homesickness for the desert, who had no choice to transform himself into an adventure, a place of torture, an uncertain and dangerous wilderness—this fool, this yearning and desperate prisoner became the inventor of "bad conscience".'[264]

It is certain that Kürten, Gein, Dahmer, West and Miyazaki all considered themselves oppressed by a narrow morality, felt persecuted by society and rubbed themselves raw on the bars of sexual constraint until they burst free with acts of murder, rape and necrophilia. But what about von Cosel, Greenlee, the Grunke brothers? What about the Swedish woman with her skeleton sex toy, her ossified dildos? Even with necrophilia, morality must be relative. Nietzsche again, 'So we modern men, because of the complicated mechanism of our "starry sky"—are defined by *differing* moral codes, our actions shine with differing colours in alternation, they are rarely clear—and there are a good many cases when we perform many-coloured actions.'[265]

If necrophilia is wrong how wrong is it? Where do a living person's rights end and a corpse's begin?

Arguing about moral calculi, William T. Vollmann hypothesizes a scenario in which a mother and child are tortured, 'Plato describes the greatest folly of all as being "that of a man who hates, not loves, what his judgment pronounces to be noble or good, while he loves and enjoys what he judges vile and wicked."'[266] Yet a necrophile pronounces what society may judge vile and wicked as noble and good. The moral calculus is inverted. Quoting Aquinas, Vollmann continues, 'As a man: "Consists in the perfection of his reason in the cognition of truth and in the regulation of his inferior appetites according to the rule of reason, for a man is a man by his rationality."'[267] However much necrophilia is an 'inferior appetite', perpetrators from Bertrand to the Swedish woman used rules of reason and rationality to satisfy their obsession. The moral calculus can be applied to Gein as well as Greenlee and the Grunkes, 'maybe there are some good people, too—isn't everyone good by his own lights?'[268] after all, 'most of us expediently rig our own moral calculuses in such a way that our actions become automatically justified in accordance with our own urgencies.'[269] Both West and Miyazaki believed their victims were 'asking for it' and that their subsequent deaths and violation were mere consequences. West perceived his victims as sex objects, flesh dolls, whereas Miyazaki believed the young girls he murdered, raped and cannibalized were hentai cartoons reified for him to enact his fantasies.

If, as Aristotle argues in *The Nicomachean Ethics*,[270] virtue is an ongoing education begun in childhood, then necrophiles (of whatever intensity) counter that education with an inverse obsessive fantasy weakening the regulative concept of morality. Necrophiliac tendencies usually begin at an early age, as in the cases of Bertrand, Kürten, Gein, Dahmer and West. If virtues are habits of the soul developed through practice, then necrophilia (and any other paraphilia) is a habit of the body also developed through practice. Aristotle, writing 100 years before Herodotus's description of Egyptian necrophilia, states that happiness (*eudaimonia*) satisfies human desire and contains no evil, that it is achieved through reason and that pleasure is a result of virtuousness and that shame results in pain. Freud sees the pleasure principle as instinctual and not a matter of rationality or reason, pleasure and pain as the main indicators of our perverse behaviour. Freud's reality principle is closer to Aristotle's idea of moral virtue and anchors the self with personal moral principles in tandem with societal ethics, whereas the pleasure principle is obsessed with instant gratification and the avoidance of psychological pain. Necrophiles go beyond the reality principle, beyond Aristotle's moral virtues, to go beyond the pleasure principle, and leap into the death drive, 'the hypothesis of a death instinct, the task of which is to lead organic life back into the inanimate state,'[271] they desire to be at one with the thing they desire. 'Freud knew it well: the death drive is opposed to the pleasure principle as well as to the reality principle. The true evil, which is the death drive, involves self-sabotage. It makes us act against our own interests.'[272]

The necrophile, from Greenlee to Gein, is driven by a desire for death and for sex; for some, like Greenlee it is out of a morbid fetishization of dead bodies, for others, like von Cosel, it is an obsessive love. The moral calculus must be adjusted in these cases to understand that, however repugnant acts of necrophilia are to the majority of society, however upsetting these bodily transgressions of loved ones must be for relatives and friends, Greenlee and von Cosel did not set out to cause pain or humiliation. It is arguable that they created their own form of happiness with their personal *eudaimonia*—good spirits. In the case of the Swedish women, the skeleton was anonymous, the bones came from all around the world. If we were to draw up a moral calculus of necrophilia would begin with the pseudonecrophiles who fantasize about necrophilia such as the Grunkes move through the Swedish woman's Paul Delvaux-like obsession with skeletons and sex, and then on to the likes of Greenlee and von Cosel, and a sharp upward curve to Gein and Bertrand and finally to the infinite series of Christie, Bundy and Dahmer.

It is only recently, in the past two decades, that necrophilia has appeared in the legislation as a specific crime. Owing to the cases of Coutts, Cooper and the Grunkes, laws have been passed making necrophilia a crime in its own right and as a consequence extending the rights of the living to the dead, because the dead cannot say yes, cannot consent to or even acquiesce to sexual activity then any such acts are deemed as rape or molestation and carry more sever sentences than previously when necrophilia was either unrecognized as a crime or grouped with other misdemeanours and punished thus—theft, vandalism, grave-robbery. In the Philippines, after the trial of Randy Uro Galvez, the Tomb Raider, legislation was introduced stating that 'whenever the crime of necrophilia is committed by two or more persons, or by any person in whose care or custody such female corpse is found, the penalty shall be death.' (see Aggrawal for a more detailed study of the legal aspects of necrophilia). What is certain is that there seems to be no increase in necrophiliac acts but a growing willingness to report the cases and a morbid and macabre interest in this extreme taboo.

There have been reports of, and YouTube videos to illustrate, necrophilia in mallard ducks, penguins, dogs, cats and toads. Websites such as Girls And Corpses mix morbid humour with scantily clad women, describing itself as 'Maxim Magazine meets Dawn Of The Dead.' A Japanese otaku website, the Sankaku Complex, specializes in anime, porn and dolls, and has designated necrophilia pages. Forums such as Goreology discuss necrophilia and posts photos and videos of dead bodies in various states of decay and mutilation. On the website Crime Scene Photos can be found images of the victims of Jack the Ripper (not a known necrophile), Ted Bundy, Ed Gein, Jerry Brudos, Andrei Chikatilo and, to this viewer, most shockingly, two young men murdered and mutilated by Jeffrey Dahmer. Necrophilia appears on television in programmes such as Irvine Welsh's *Wedding Belles*, *Family Guy*, *Criminal Minds*, *Nip/Tuck*, the *CSI* franchise and in the movies *Freddy vs. Jason*, *Weekend At Bernie's*, *Clerks* and *Quills* (about de Sade). From the above list it is apparent that necrophilia is treated as an investigative forensic subject, as a platform for morbid humour or as a means to shock the viewer. Irvine Welsh uses necrophilia to shock us, disgust us but also to make us laugh.

There was nothing like the sight of a stiff to give Freddy Royle a stiffie.

- Bit bashed about this one, Glen, the path lab technician explained, as he wheeled the body into the hospital mortuary.

Freddy was finding it hard to maintain steady breathing. He examined the corpse.

- She's bain a roight pretty un n arl, he rasped in his Somerset drawl, – caar accident oi presumes?

- Yeah, poor cow. M25. Lost too much blood by the time they cut her out of the pile-up, Glen mumbled uncomfortably. He was feeling a bit sick. Usually a stiff was just a stiff to him, and he had seen them in all conditions. Sometimes though, when it was someone young, or someone whose beauty could still be evidenced from the three-dimensional photograph of flesh they had left behind, the sense of the waste and futility of it all just fazed him. This was such an occasion.

One of the dead girl's legs was lacerated to the bone. Freddy ran his hand up the perfect one. It felt smooth. – Still a bit wahrm n arl, he observed, – bit too waarm for moi tastes if the truth be told. [273]

The taboo makes us reacts with laughter or disgust, a pornography of bodily functions and response.

There are many cases that have not been discussed because of the similarity of the acts to other acts documented or the lack of evidence that necrophilia actually occurred. And, again, these necrophiliac acts range from the frottage of 18-year-old Alisa Massaro who, it was claimed in 2013, along with two of her sexual partners strangled two men in order for her to be able to lie on top of them, ala Karen Greenlee, and bring herself to orgasm. Or that of a Michigan pastor who killed his fiancee's daughter in 2012 to realize his necrophiliac fantasies. Or the Egyptian court, which in 2012 introduced a bill legalizing "farewell intercourse" so that men could have sex with their dead wives for up to six hours after their death. It is also evident that necrophilia is a worldwide phenomenon, Thor Nis Christiansen (Danish), Roderick Jones (American), Lam Kor-wan (Chinese), Issei Sagawa (Japanese), Moninder Singh Pandher and Surendra Koli (Indian), Andrei Chikatilo (Russian), Serhiy Tkach (Ukrainian) and Eli Ulayuk (Inuit). All homicidal or regular necrophiles, and some, like Chikatilo who indulged in necrophilia as part of his lust murders. But it is with a study of a Frenchman, Nico Claux, that I will conclude this book on necrophilia and necrophiles.

13

Necroclusion

Nico Claux[274] shared many similarities with Sergeant Bertrand, Ted Bundy and Jeffrey Dahmer. After his arrest in November 1994 on suspicion of being a serial killer who targeted gay men, police discovered vertebrae and bones used as everyday and art objects in his apartment. As in the case of Miyakazki, the detectives also found videos of horror and sadomasochistic movies. Like Dahmer, Claux kept bags of blood in his fridge and hardcore porn magazine on his bookshelves. Unlike Dahmer, Claux had not collected the blood from his victims but, like so many other necrophiles, had worked as a mortuary assistant and had collected the blood from the morgue. He had necrophiliac and cannibalistic fantasies and had had stolen bones from several Paris cemeteries and had cut strips of flesh from the bodies in the morgue to cook and eat. 'Sacrifice replaces the ordered life of the animal with a blind convulsion of its organs. So also with the erotic convulsion; it gives free rein to extravagant organs whose blind activity goes on beyond the considered will of the lovers. Their considered will is followed by the animal activity of these swollen organs. They are animated by a violence outside the control of reason to yield to the breaking storm.'[275]

Police were suspicious of Claux's testimony, believing him to be a fantasist with an obsession with vampires and pornography. Born in Cameroon to French parents, Claux, like many serial killers, was an only child whose parents showed little or no love towards him. The family moved from Cameroon to London and then to France and the solitary boy became interested in vampires, werewolves, zombies and the occult, and death became an obsession after his grandfather died from a cerebral embolism while he was present. The actual death of his grand-father merged with the cult of death the 10-year-old Claux had created and he began to attend wakes and habituate cemeteries and mortuaries. 'But places are dead bodies: their spaces, their tombs, their extended masses, and our bodies coming and going among them, among ourselves.'[276]

Because the family moved regularly, Claux found it difficult to make friends, his obsession with death could not have helped, and he became more insular and isolated and here the 'germs of perversion'[277] and 'infantile seeds of perversion'[278] began, along with a feeling of hatred for other people. At the age of 16, the family returned to Paris and Claux began frequenting the same cemeteries in which Sergeant Bertrand had disinterred, mutilated and ravaged corpses—Montparnasse and Père Lachaise among others. Here death and sex are united in a 'twofold evolution tend[ing] to make the flesh into the root of all evil, shifting the most important moment of transgression from the act itself to the stirrings—so difficult to perceive and formulate—of desire.'[279]

Claux began to break into mausoleums and tombs using homemade locks and picks. Once inside, he felt powerful, in charge, the king of the dead, a sadistic despot of corpses.

'What is a criminal after all? A criminal is someone who breaks the pact, who breaks it from time to time whenever he needs or wants to, when his interest dictates, when in a moment of violence or blindness the motive of his interest prevails despite the most elementary rational calculation. The criminal is a temporary despot, a despot of the moment, through blindness, fantasy, passion, or whatever. By contrast, the despot asserts the predominance of his interest and will; he makes it prevail perma-nently. The despot is a criminal by his status whereas the criminal is a despot by accident. When I say by status I am exaggerating because the despot cannot have any status in society. The despot can promote his will over the entire social body only through a permanent state of violence. The despot is therefore someone who—beyond status and the law, but in a way that is completely bound up with his very existence—permanently exercises and advances his interest in a criminal way. The despot is the permanent outlaw, the individual without social ties. The despot is the man alone.[280]

Claux's obsessions were death and sex, and the sex was becoming more sadistic, more violent, his ability to break into mausoleums and not be detected increased his belief that he was untouchable, above and beyond the law and any moral reckoning, any ethical constraints. Freud argues that 'Some take perversion perfectly for granted, just as a normal person will take the direction of his libido to be quite natural, and keenly stress their equality with normal people. But others reject the fact of their inversion and perceive it as a morbid compulsion.'[281]

This feeling of power and desire led Claux to the Passy Cemetery across the Seine from the Eiffel Tower and home to the remains of Octave Mirbeau author of *The Torture Garden*.

'You're obliged to pretend respect for people and institutions you think absurd. You live attached in a cowardly fashion to moral and social conventions you despise, condemn, and know lack all foundation. It is that permanent contradiction between your ideas and desires and all the dead formalities and vain pretenses of your civilization which makes you sad, troubled and unbalanced. In that intolerable conflict you lose all joy of life and all feeling of personality, because at every moment they suppress and restrain and check the free play of your powers. That's the poisoned and mortal wound of the civilized world.'[282]

Once inside the cemetery he entered a mausoleum containing the bodies of a Russian family relocated to Paris after the 1917 revolution. Claux opened one of the coffins, inhaled the odour of decay and embalming fluid, and experienced 'a religion of breath ... of impalpable touch, a religion of the word, of proferring, of exhaling—a deleterious odor of the dead, with perfumes pleasing to the One Eternal, an odor of sanctity.'[283]

Inside the coffin, Claux saw the shrouded body of an old woman, he tried to unclothe the corpse but it was stuck down with bodily fluids and embalming chemicals. The skin was petrified, the teeth yellow, the eyes were missing from the orbits.

'The body's like a pure spirit: it keeps completely to itself and inside itself, in a single point. Break that point, and the body dies. The point's situated between the eyes, between the ribs, in the middle of the liver, all around the skull, in the midst of the femoral artery, and in lots of other places, too. The body's a collection of spirits.'[284]

A vertiginous feeling overwhelmed Claux, he took a screw-driver from his tool kit and preceded to stab the corpse in the stomach and through the ribcage in a similar way to the method used by Peter Sutcliffe to kill and mutilate his victims. After this initial desecration, Claux continued his symbolic necrophilia in other cemeteries around Paris.

Like Sergeant Bertrand 130 years before him, Claux joined the French Army and spent his time planning murders. His army career only lasted a year and he left wanting to become a mortician but his application to study embalming was declined. Desiring to be near dead bodies, he found a position as a morgue attendant at Saint Vincent-de-Paul Hospital in Paris where he assisted in autopsies. 'An anatomy of configurations, of the plasticity of what we'd have to call states of body, ways of being, bearing, breathings, paces, staggerings, sufferings, pleasures, coats, windings, brushings, masses. Bodies, to begin with, are masses, masses offered with nothing to be articulated about them, nothing to link them to, whether a discourse or a story: palms, cheeks, wombs, buttocks. Even an eye is a mass, as are tongue and ear-lobe.'[285]

Claux became fascinated with body parts, organs and skulls at the various hospitals he worked at. Besides assisting in autopsies, he cleaned the mortuary slabs, prepared bodied for viewing by relatives, worked as a stretcher-bearer, anything to be in proximity to a corpse. Left alone with the dead bodies, he began to excise strips of flesh and muscle and took the home to eat raw or cook. It was also during work in the hospital that he began to steel bags of blood from the blood bank, these he would make into a morbid milkshake using protein powders or human ashes.

These acts were not enough for Claux and his fantasies became more violent. Over Minitel (a pre-WWW service), Claux made contact with a 34-year-old man called Thierry Bissonnier and they agreed to meet for sadomasochistic sex. Claux took with him a gun and on entering the apartment shot Thierry through the eye. After searching the flat, Claux discovered that Thierry was still alive and shot him again in the back of the head. But Thierry wouldn't die. After eating some cookies while watching Thierry, he then shot him in the back and smashed a plant pot on his head. After getting rid of any incriminating evidence, Claux stole personal items to make the act look like a burglary. Among the items stolen by Claux was a cheque book and a driver's licence, which he used to buy a VCR; however, the shop assistant became suspicious and notified the police but Claux had already fled.

After being apprehended, Claux confessed to the crime and to his desecration of tombs and cannibalism; he denied any sexual motive, claiming he just wanted to murder someone, anyone. Psychiatrists who examined Claux diagnosed him as having a borderline psychotic personality disorder, necrophiliac and sexually sadistic tendencies and schizophrenia very similar to the psychiatric notes made on Miyazaki.

On the 9th of May 1997, Claux stood trial for the murder of Thierry Bissonnier. The jury was shown photographs of the crime scene and of Claux's apartment—a union of Gein's and Dahmer's homes—in order to show that Claux's fantasy world had tipped over into reality and was responsible for a number of murders in Paris. Like Sergeant Bertrand, Peter Kürten and Friedrich Haarmann before him, Claux was a dubbed 'a real-life vampire.'

Eventually, the jurors took only three hours to find Claux guilty of premeditated murder, armed robbery and fraud and he was sentenced to 12 years in prison. After four years in Fleury-Merogis prison he was transferred to Maison Centrale Poissy where he claimed he made contact with serial killers. While there, he studied computer programming and spent his spare time in the gym and painting. Claux was incarcerated for seven years and four months and released in March 2002.

There is no doubt that Nico Claux is and was a fantasist. His pseudonecrophilia may have led him to murder Thierry Bissonnier but there is no concrete evidence that he sexually interfered with the body or the bodies he may or may not have disinterred. The psychiatric reports branded him a necrophile because of his obsession with death and dead bodies. Claux achieved minor celebrity status after his release because of his tales of grave-robbery, sadomasochism and a fascination with serial killers, subjects he posts on his website. His paintings include portraits of Ed Gein, Ted Bundy and Jeffrey Dahmer, He welcomes the Vampire of Paris tag and travels the world promoting the occult, fetishism, tattooing and Gothism. When asked in an interview 'what killers stick in your mind?' he mentioned Ed Gein and also that he admired Sergeant Bertrand.

We all live a psychosexual life. Not all of us realize that life. And maybe that's a good thing. Most pseudonecrophiles live a life of blameless fantasy in which death is a substitute for any other fetish. Regular necrophiles are few and desire the dead through an obsessional need for human contact, even if the human is dead, and this like other perversions is most likely triggered in childhood, although to a far lesser degree than sadism, masochism and the other paraphilias. Foucault would argue that necrophilia was but one of many instances of humankind's 'manifold sexualities' that, 'The nineteenth century and our own have been rather the age of multiplication: a dispersion of sexualities, a strengthening of their disparate forms, a multiple implantation of "perversions." Our epoch has initiated sexual heterogeneities.'[286] Freud would agree, believing necrophilia—in particular the pseudo and regular kinds—were part of our polymorphous perversity, that necrophilia is a matter of transgression and a degree of inversion. '"Perverse" is then the absence of disgust in a context where reactions of disgust and repression are normally expected; it is the untimely persistence of infantile libido, the breakdown of the civilized devaluation of smells, excrement, mouth and anus (a devaluation serving to promote purely genital sexuality).'[287] If that is the case then it is one of the 'peripheral sexualities. Whence the setting apart of the 'unnatural' as a specific dimension in the field of sexuality. This kind of activity assumed an autonomy with regard to the other condemned forms such as adultery or rape (and the latter was condemned less and less): to marry a close relative or practice sodomy, to seduce a nun or engage in sadism, to deceive one's wife or violate cadavers, became things that were essentially different.'[288]

In researching this book I have come to the conclusion that pseudonecrophilia is the domain of fantasists and occultists, people interested in morbid pornography, gothic art, horror films and novels. So-called regular necrophiles are rare and the majority of them are drawn to the act through proximity, availability and curiosity; very few practice necrophilia exclusively, most are unable to establish sexual relationships with other people of either sex and practice necrophilia along with other paraphilias such as bestiality and sadomasochism. The alleged necrophilia of ex-BBC disc jockey Jimmy Savile (if found to be true) constitutes a fragment of his wider biastophilia or raptophilia, and his desire to rape women, underage children (of both sexes), brain-damaged patients and dying residents of hospitals and hospices. In Irvine Welsh's "Lorraine Goes to Livingston," in *Ecstasy*, the character of Freddy Royle, a thinly disguised portrait of Savile, uses his power and contacts to satisfy his lusts.

'Yes, the trustees knew all about Freddy Royle, Glen reflected bitterly. They knew the real secrets of the chat-show host, the authors of several books, including *Howzat! – Freddy Royle On Cricket*, *Freddy Royle's Somerset*, *Somerset With a Z: The Wit of the West Country*, *West Country Walks With Freddy Royle* and *Freddy Royle's 101 Magic Party Tricks*. Yes, those trustee bastards knew what this distinguished friend, this favorite caring, laconic uncle to the nation did with the stiffs they got in here. The thing was, Freddy brought millions of pounds into the place with his fund-raising activities. This brought kudos to the trustees, and made St Hubbin's Hospital a flagship for the arm's-length trusts from the NHS. All they had to do was keep schtumm and indulge Sir Freddy with the odd body.'[289]

In England's Darkness, Stephen Barber allies Savile with Peter Sutcliffe, imagining a meeting between the two men.

'He evoked—deliriously, in bursts, as though speaking in glossolalia—a meeting that had taken place, in October 1988, at the Broadmoor hospital for the criminally insane, between the two now-dead but still-legendary 'Kings of Leeds', Peter Sutcliffe and Jimmy Savile, during Savile's era as that hospital's de-facto director, having seized power from his ostensible advisory role, at a seminal moment when, due to malfunctions of its administrative regime, the insane had ruled that asylum, sweeping-aside its directors. The two Kings of Leeds had met for profound discussions of the future, in a palatial, thickly-curtained annex of the asylum, first embracing one another warmly, then stood together, Sutcliffe's head turned attentively to Savile, two eager interpreters beside them, as though only irreconcilable idioms of madness could be voiced. But they remained silent, as though in anticipation of being photographed, like two dictators, though no image was to be made of that meeting, and its memory subsisted solely in the pixellated hallucinations of a soon-to-be-culled rebel boy, standing in front of the pornography cinema's screen, in the semen-preserved grandeur of the Assembly Rooms, his delirium now drained, but his throat still convulsing with the effort to expectorate, at last, a myth, an origin.'[290]

Savile may have committed necrophiliac acts; in 1990 in *Q Magazine*, he told the interviewer about his obsession with dead bodies, while at Stoke Mandeville Hospital, he had volunteered to take dead bodies to the morgue. He may have been, like Karen Greenlee, an opportunistic necrophile (as he had been an opportunistic rapist). Yet he may also have been a fantasist and the rumours surrounding his crimes (see the Welsh extract) projections of his paedophilia in order to metamorphose him into the ultimate contemporary sexual monster. His inclusion in Barber's apocalyptic novel and his (imagined) meeting with Peter Sutcliffe promotes/demotes Savile to the status of postmodern demon, sexual predator of hospitals, television studios, prisons and asylums—JG Ballard died three years before the Savile scandal broke but Savile retrospectively haunts the Ballardian landscape.

Of the homicidal-necrophiles such as Peter Kürten, Ed Gein, Ted Bundy and Jeffrey Dahmer, necrophilia became part of their polymorphous perversity, their manifold sexualities, their heterogeneous libidos. For the majority of us, 'Bound in with the selfhood of the physical body, most of us believe, there lives a moral, mental, spiritual and emotional being. That is one reason why it feels so odd to me to gaze upon a corpse.'[291] For serial killers like Bundy and Dahmer, necrophilia was a sexual component of their perversions and not the reason they killed women and men. The necrophile who exhumes dead bodies in order to have sex with them is a near-mythical thing, even Sergeant Bertrand mostly masturbated over the entrails. Similar to the proliferation of specialist magazine, websites and television channels, it is a matter of media targeting,

'"Targeting," said the male columnist, who was about twenty-eight and experimentally bearded, with a school-dinner look about him. The column the male columnist wrote was sociopolitical. "Come on, this isn't America. Where the magazine market is completely balkanized. Where, you know, they have magazines," he said, already looking round the table to garner any smiles that might soon be cropping up, "for the twice-divorced South Moluccan scuba diver."'[292]

And necrophilia finds its own abhorrent balkanized place in the myriad of paraphilias—from abasiophilia, a sexual attraction to people with impaired mobility, to zoosadism, sexual excitement from watching animals in pain or causing them pain. (Some people would argue that the last paraphilia is a more malignant perversion than necrophilia, as is the torture of humans.) Like the majority of paraphilias, necrophilia is rare and targeted by the press because it is shocking, involves death and sex and excites our morbid curiosity but Sergeant Bertrand is unlikely to have a prime-time television show produced based on his exploits as the werewolf-vampire-demon-based shows *Buffy the Vampire Slayer*, *Angel*, *True Blood* and *Being Human*.

If, as Freudians contest, all love objects are substitute mother figures, then the homicidal-necrophile perpetually kills his mother to have sex with her in order to be reborn as an 'other' who would not then become a necrophile. If that is the case, we are all necrophiles to a certain extent because '[i]n the span of its lifetime, the body is also a dead body, the body of a dead person, this dead person I am when alive. Dead or alive, neither dead nor alive, I am the opening, the tomb or the mouth, the one inside the other.'[293]

Endnotes

1—Necroduction

1   Richard von Krafft-Ebing, *Psychopathia Sexualis*, trans. Franklin S. Klaf (New York, 1998), p. 65.

2   Gilles Deleuze & Félix Guattari, *Anti-Oedipus: Capitalism and Schizophrenia*, trans. Robert Hurley, Mark Seem, and Helen R. Lane (London, 2004), p. 329.

3   *Psychopathia Sexualis*, p. 68.

4   Gilles Deleuze, *Difference and Repetition*, trans. Paul Patton (London, 1994), p. 20.

5   Gilles Deleuze and Félix Guattari, *A Thousand Plateaus: Capitalism and schizophrenia*, trans. Brian Massumi, (Minneapolis, 1987), p. 439.

6   Quoted in Nick Land, *The Thirst for Annihilation, Georges Bataille and Virulent Nihilism* (London, 1992), p. 49.

7   Wallace Stevens, *The Collected Poems* (New York, 1982), p. 339.

8   J.G. Ballard, *Crash,* (London, 2008), p. 6.

9   F.T. Marinetti, *Critical Writings*, trans. Doug Thompson (New York, 2006), p. 13

10 *A Thousand Plateaus: Capitalism and Schizophrenia*, p. 276.

11 Heidegger, Martin, *Being and Time*, trans. John Macquarrie and Edward Robinson (New York, 1962), p 51.

12 Graham Harman, *Towards Speculative Realism* (Ropley, Hants, 2010), p. 20.

13 J.G. Ballard, *The Atrocity Exhibition* (Revised edition: London, 2006), p. 82.

14 *The Atrocity Exhibition*, p.92.

15 Thomas Metzinger, *The Ego Tunnel: the science of the mind and the myth of the self* (New York, 2009, pp. 100-101.

16 Gilles Deleuze and Félix Guattari, p. 356.

17 *The Atrocity Exhibition*, p.95.

18   *The Atrocity Exhibition*, p.101.
19   *The Atrocity Exhibition*, p.112.
20   Slavoz Žižek, *Violence* (New York, 2008), p. 20.
21   *The Atrocity Exhibition*, p.120.
22   *The Atrocity Exhibition*, p.120.
23   *The Atrocity Exhibition*, p.117.
24   *The Atrocity Exhibition*, p.120.
25   Gilles Deleuze, *Difference and Repetition*, p. 299.
26   *The Atrocity Exhibition*, p.53.

2—Necrophilia—Deathinition

27   William T. Vollmann, *The Rainbow Stories* (New York, 1989), p. 297.
28   Supervert, *Necrophilia Variations* (USA, 2005), p. 1.
29   *Necrophilia Variations*, p. 194.
30   Charles Baudelaire, 'A Martyred Woman,' from *Selected Poems of Charles Baudelaire*, translated by Geoffrey Wagner, (New York, 1974).
31   American Psychiatric Association, *Diagnostic and Statistical Manual of Mental* (4th ed., text rev.). (Washington DC, 2000) p. 535.
32   Michel Foucault, *The History of Sexuality, An Introduction, Volume I.* trans. Robert Hurley (New York, 1990), p 160.
33   *A Thousand Plateaus: Capitalism and Schizophrenia*, p. 275.
34   *Violence*, pp. 164-5.
35   Jo Nesbø, *The Bat*, (London, 2012), p. 109.
36   See Paul E. Mullen Michele Pathé, and Rosemary Purcell, *Stalkers and Their Victims* (Cambridge, 2000).
37   *Violence*, p. 61.
38   Michael Marshall, *Straw Men*, (New York, 2002), p. 106.
39   *The Atrocity Exhibition*, p. 31.
40   Sigmund Freud, 'Fetishism', *The Complete Psychological Works of Sigmund Freud, Vol. 21*, trans. James Strachey (London, 2001), pp. 152-158.

41 *A Thousand Plateaus: Capitalism and Schizophrenia*, p. 129.

42 *The Atrocity Exhibition*, p. 156.

43 *A Thousand Plateaus: Capitalism and Schizophrenia*, p. 259.

44 Donald Winnicott, 'Transitional Objects and Transitional Phenomena—a Study of the First Not-me Possession,' *International Journal of Psycho-Analysis*, 34, 89-97 (1953).

45 *A Thousand Plateaus: Capitalism and Schizophrenia*, p. 129.

46 *Anti-Oedipus*, p. 267.

47 See: Anil Aggrawal, *Necrophilia: Forensic and Medico-Legal Aspects* (Boca Raton, 2011). All quotes from early case studies are taken from this excellent study.

48 See: Chapter 3, *Necrophilia: Forensic and Medico-Legal Aspects*.

49 See: Havelock Ellis, *Studies in the Psychology of Sex, Volume V: Erotic Symbolism, The Mechanism of Detumescence, The Psychic State in Pregnancy*, (Philadelphia, 1923).

50 See: A. A. Brill, *Necrophilia—Part I. J. Criminal Psychopathology*, 1941;2(4) pp. 433–443.

51 Ruth Rendell, *Thirteen Steps Down* (London, 2005), p. 133.

52 Poppy Z. Brite, *Exquisite Corpse* (London, 1996), p. 66.

53 Edgar Allan Poe, *Poetry and Tales* (New York, 1984) p. 276

54 See: Erich Fromm, *The Anatomy of Human Destructiveness* (New York, 1973).

55 See Chapter 2, *Necrophilia: Forensic and Medico-Legal Aspects*.

56 'Sexual attraction to corpses: a psychiatric review of necrophilia', Bull. Am Acad. Psychiatry Law. 1989; 17 (2), pp. 153–163.

57 See: Chapter 4, *Necrophilia: Forensic and Medico-Legal Aspects*.

58 *Straw Men*, p. 208.

3 —NecroHysteria—A Short History

59 Herodotus, *The History*, trans. David Greene (Chicago, 1987) p. 167.

60 Simon Critchley, *The Book of Dead Philosophers* (London, 2008), p. 16.

61 Poppy Z. Brite, *Exquisite corpse* (London, 1996), p. 15.

62 *The Book of Dead Philosophers*, p. 279.

63 *The Book of Dead Philosophers*, p. xii.

64 Cormac McCarthy, *Child of God* (London, 2010), p. 87.

65 Karl Tanzler von Cosel, 'The Secret of Elena's Tomb,' *Fantastic Adventures*, September 1947, (Chicago, 1947). This ghosted novella followed 'The Mad Scientist' a short story by *Psycho* author Robert Bloch. http://www.unz.org/Pub /FantasticAdventures-1947sep-00008

66 'The Secret of Elena's Tomb'.

67 David Foster Wallace, *Both Flesh and Not*, (London, 2012), p. 46.

68 See Tom Swicegood, *Von Cosel*, (Lincoln, 2003), Ben Harrison, *Undying love: the true story of a passion that defied death* (New York, 2001)

69 'The Secret of Elena's Tomb'.

70 Slavoj Žižek, *Violence* (New York, 2008), p. 63.

71 George Bataille, *Erotism: Death & Sensuality*, trans. Mary Dalwood (San Francisco, 1986), p. 92.

72 Sigmund Freud, *The Psychology of Love*, trans. Shaun Whiteside (London, 2006), p. 39.

73 Jim Morton, 'The Unrepentant Necrophile: An Interview with Karen Greenlee,' *Apocalypse culture: volume 1*, ed., Adam Parfrey (Portland, 1990), p. 28.

74 *Nekromantik* (1987) and *Nekromantik 2* (1991) directed by Jörg Buttgereit.

75 Georges Bataille, *Story of the Eye* (London, 2001), p. 34.

76 *The Psychology of Love*, p. 130.

77 See Sigmund Freud, 'Totem and Taboo and Other Works,' *The Complete Psychological works of Sigmund Freud*, Vol. 13, trans. James Strachey (London, 2001)

78 See Mary Weismantel, 'Moche Sex Pots: Reproduction and Temporality Ancient South America,' *American Anthropologist*, Vol. 6, No. 3, September 2004, pp. 495-505.

Endnotes

79 Grant Morrison, *Supergods* (London 2011), p.136.
80 Quintus of Smyrna, *The Trojan Epic: Posthomerica*, trans. Alan James (Baltimore, 2007), pp. 3-24.
81 Parthenius, *Love Stories 2*, http://www.theoi.com/Text/Parthenius2.html#31. See Pierre Grimal, *The dictionary of classical mythology* (Oxford, 1996), p.137.
82 Aryeh Kasher and Eliezer Witztum, *King Herod: a persecuted persecutor: a case study in psychohistory and psychobiography*, trans. Karen Gold (Berlin, 2007), p.171.
83 Flavius Josephus, *Jewish Antiquities* (London, 2006), p. 662.
84 *Anti-Oedipus*, p. 27.
85 *Anti-Oedipus*, p. 26.
86 *Metaphysical Poetry*, ed. Colin Burrow (London, 2006), p. 226.
87 Thomas Vaughan, *The Works of Thomas Vaughan*, ed. Arthur Edward Waite (Whitefish MT, 2010), p. 446.
88 *The Works of Thomas Vaughan*, p. xli.
89 *Metaphysical Poetry*, p. 198.
90 Marquis de Sade, *The Complete Marquis de Sade*, Vol. 1., trans. Dr Paul J. Gillette (Los Angeles, 2005), p. 134.
91 *The Complete Marquis de Sade*, p. 226.
92 Michel Foucault, *The History of Sexuality*, p. 149.
93 Maurice Blanchot, *The Writing of the Disaster*, trans. Ann Smock (Lincoln, 2005), p. 45.
94 Slavoj Žižek, *The Parallax View*, (Cambridge MA, 2009), p. 93.
95 John Phillips, *Sade: The Libertine Novels* (London, 2001), p. 140.
96 E. D. Steele, *Palmerston and Liberalism, 1855-1865* A (Cambridge, 1991), p. 225.
97 Jacques Lacan, *The Seminars of Jacques Lacan: book VII, the ethics of psychoanalysis 1959-1960*, ed. Jacques-Alain Miller, trans. Dennis Porter (New York, 1997), p. 282.
98 *Psychopathia Sexualis*, p. 351.

99   Iwan Block, *The Sexual Life of Our Time: Its Relations to Modern Civilization*, Trans. M. Eden Paul (London, 1909), pp. 647-648.

100 See Masahiro Mori, *The Buddha in the Robot: A Robot Engineer's Thoughts on Science and Religion*, trans. Charles S. Terry (Tokyo, 1981).

101 Kaja Silverman, *Male Subjectivity at the Margins* (London, 1992), p. 187.

102 *Male Subjectivity at the Margins*, p. 186.

103 Allison de Fren, 'The Exquisite Corpse: Disarticulations Of The Artificial Female,' unpublished doctoral dissertation, USC, 2008, p. 8.

104 *The Book of Dead Philosophers*, p. 7.

105 Diogenes Laertius, *Lives of Eminent Philosophers*, Volume 1, trans. Robert Drew Hicks (Cambridge, 1972), p. 101.

106 Slavoj Žižek, *How to Read Lacan*, (London, 2006), pp. 100-101.

107 Stewart Home, ' The Necrocard: Anyone For Sex After Death?' http://www.stewarthomesociety.org/neoism/necro.htm

108 See Patricia MacCormack, 'Necrosexuality,' *Rhizomes* 11/12, fall 2005/spring 2006, http://www.rhizomes.net/issue11/maccormack/index.html

4—Necronaut—Sergeant Bertrand

109 Quotes and details of Bertrand's crimes taken from L. Thoinot, *Medicolegal Aspects of Moral Offenses*, trans. Arthur W. Weysse (Philadelphia, 1923), pp. 449-458.

110 Jacques Lacan, *Four Fundamental Concepts of Psycho-Analysis*, ed. Jacques-Alain Miller and trans. Alan Sheridan (New York, 1978), p. 112.

111 *Violence*, pp. 155-156.

112 Karl Marx, *The Revolutions of 1848*, (Harmondsworth, 1973), pp. 129-134.

113 *The History of Sexuality*, p. 69.

114 Available at http://www.senate.gov.ph/lis/bill_res.aspx?con
gress=14&q=SBN1038
115 William Shakespeare, *Hamlet*, V. 1. 249-50.
116 Jacques Lacan, 'Desire and the Interpretation of Desire in
Hamlet,' trans. James Hulbert, Yale *French Studies* 55-56
(1977), pp 11-52.
117 See Erich Wulffen, *Enzyklopadie de Modernen Kriminalistik*,
(Berlin, 1910).
118 For details of Bertrand's crimes and case, see Dr Alexis
Épaulard, *Vampirisme, Nécrophilie, Nécrosadisme, Nécrophagie*
(Lyons, 1901).
119 Enrico Ferri, *Criminal Sociology* (1899) available from
http://www.gutenberg.org/ebooks/477

5—NecroGermania

120 Details of the lives and crimes of Kürten, Haarmann,
Grossmann, and Denke, are from various sources, my
descriptions should be considered an amalgamation of
available texts, including: Theodor Lessing, Karl Berg,
George Godwin, *Monsters of Weimar: The Stories of Fritz
Haarmann and Peter Kurten*, trans. Mo Croasdale (London,
1993); Maria Tatar, *Lustmord: Sexual Murder in Weimar
Germany* (Princeton, 1997); Katherine Ramsland, *The Mind of
a Murderer: Privileged Access to the Demons That Drive Extreme
Violence* (Santa Barbara, 2011). Websites:
http://www.trutv.com/library/crime/serial_killers/history/k
urten/index_1.html, http://www.trutv.com/library/crime/
serial_killers/history/haarman/index_1.html, and relevant
Wikipedia pages.
121 Octave Mirbeau, *The Torture Garden*, trans. Alvah Bessie
(London, 2008), p. 83.
122 Karl Marx and Friedrich Engels, 'The Holy Family,' *Complete
Works Vol. 4*, trans. Richard Dixon and Clement Dutts, first
published 1845. Available from http://www.marxists.org

/archive/marx/works/1845/holy-family/index.htm
123 Franz Kafka, *Metamorphosis and Other Stories*, trans. Michael Hoffman (London, 2007), p. 49.
124 *Metamorphosis and Other Stories*, p. 50.
125 Max Brod, *Franz Kafka: A Biography*, trans. G. Humphreys Roberts and Richard Winston (New York, 1995), p. 129.
126 Adolf Hitler, *The Essential Hitler: Speeches and Commentary*, trans. Max Domarus (Wauconda, 2007), p. 262.
127 Peter Watson, *The German Genius*, (London, 2010) p. 568.
128 Sigmund Freud, Civilization and Its Discontents, (London, 2004), p. 60.
129 *The Pervert's Guide to the Cinema*, dir. Sophie Fiennes, released January 2009. Author transcription.
130 See Sigmund Freud, The Dissection of the Psychical Personality, *New Introductory Lectures on Psychoanalysis*, trans. James Strachey (New York, 1995) pp. 71- 100.
131 Sigmund Freud, *Civilization and Its Discontents*, trans. James Strachey (New York, 2005), p. 141.
132 Sigmund Freud, 'The Ego and the Id,' *The Standard Edition of the Complete Psychological Works of Sigmund Freud, Vol. 19*, trans. James Strachey (London, 2001), p. 40.
133 'The Ego and the Id,' p. 41.

6—NecroCinema—Prohibition, Inhibition, Exhibition

134 For a further analysis of *The Texas Chain Saw* massacre, see Robin Wood, 'An Introduction to the American Horror Film', *Planks of Reason: Essays on the Horror Film*, Barry Keith Grant, ed. (Metuchen, NJ, 1984); and Naomi Merritt, 'Cannibalistic Capitalism and other American Delicacies: A Bataillean Taste of *The Texas Chain Saw Massacre*,' *Film-Philosophy*, Vol 14, No 1 (2010)
135 *The Silence of the Lambs*, dir. Jonathan Demme, 1991. Author transcription.
136 Gordon Burn, *Happy Like Murderers* (London, 1999), pp. 105-

06.

137 Graham Harman, *Prince of Networks: Bruno Latour and Metaphysics*, (Melbourne, 2009), p. 24.

138 Vladimir Nabokov, *Speak, Memory* (London, 2000), p.5.

7—NecroAmerica

139 For details about the life and crimes of Ed Gein see Howard Schechter, *Deviant* (New York, 1989), and Paul Anthony Woods, *Ed Gein—Psycho!* (New York, 1995).

140 Slavoj Žižek, *How to Read Lacan* (New York, 2007) available at http://www.lacan.com/zizekthing.htm

141 Bret Easton Ellis, *American Psycho*, (London, 2006) p. 92.

142 *Anti-Oedipus*, pp. 329-330.

143 *Anti-Oedipus*, p. 330.

144 *Anti-Oedipus*, p. 330.

145 Slavoj Žižek, *How to Read Lacan* (New York, 2007)

146 Gaston Bachelard, *The Poetics of Space*, trans. Maria Jolas (Boston, 1994), Foreword, p. viii.

8—NecroBritannia

147 *The History of Sexuality*, p. 83.

148 *Happy Like Murderers*, p. 297.

149 *Happy Like Murderers*, p. 297.

150 Ludovic Kennedy, *Ten Rillington Place* (London, 1961), p. 46.

151 For further information on the life and crimes of John Christie, see John Eddowes, *The Two Killers of Rillington Place* (New York, 1995) Ludovic, Kennedy, *Ten Rillington Place* (London, 1961), Keith Simpson, *Forty Years of Murder* London, 2008), and the movie *Ten Rillington Place* directed by Richard Fleischer (1970).

152 Colin Wilson, *A Criminal History of Mankind* (London, 2005), p. 19.

153 *A Criminal History of Mankind*, p. 563.

154 *The Poetics of Space*, p. 78.

155 *The Poetics of Space*, p. 79.
156 Charles Baudelaire, 'The Punishment of Pride,' *Poems of Baudelaire,* trans. Roy Campbell, (New York, 1952). Available – http://fleursdumal.org/poem/115
157 'The Punishment of Pride,' *Poems of Baudelaire.*

9 — NecroSuperstar

158 Ted Bundy is somewhat of a superstar in the firmament/fundament of serial killers. Details on his life and crimes are detailed on many websites. Below is a list of the best of the secondary material: Robert D., Keppel, *Riverman: Ted Bundy & I Hunt for the Green River Killer* (New York, 1995),Stephen G. Michaud and Hugh Aynesworth, *Ted Bundy: Conversations with a Killer* (Authorlink Press, 2000), Ann Rule, *The Stranger Beside Me* (New York, 1989); plus see websites http://www.trutv.com/library/crime/serial_killers/notorious/bundy/index_1.html and http://en.wikipedia.org/wiki/Ted_Bundy.
159 Stephen G. Michaud and Hugh Aynesworth, *The Only Living Witness: The True Story of Serial Sex Killer Ted Bundy* (Irving, 1999), p. 335.
160 Georges Bataille, *Visions of Excess: Selected Writings, 1927-1939*, trans. Allan Stoekl with Carl R. Lovitt and Donald M. Leslie Jr. (Minneapolis MN, 1985), p. 94.
161 Julia Kristeva, *Powers of Horror: An Essay on Abjection*, trans. Leon S. Roudiez, (New York, 1982), p.6.
162 Interview transcribed by author — clip 1 audiotape available: http://www.kirotv.com/news/4182402/detail.html
163 *Powers of Horror: An Essay on Abjection*, p.6.
164 Geoffrey Roche, *Black Sun: Bataille on Sade*, University of Auckland.
165 *Powers of Horror: An Essay on Abjection*, p.7.
166 *Black Sun: Bataille on Sade.*
167 *American Psycho*, p. 241.

168 *Powers of Horror: An Essay on Abjection*, p.8.
169 *Black Sun: Bataille on Sade*.
170 *Powers of Horror: An Essay on Abjection*, p. 8.
171 *American Psycho*, pp. 394-396.
172 *Powers of Horror: An Essay on Abjection*, p. 8.
173 *Black Sun: Bataille on Sade*.
174 *Powers of Horror: An Essay on Abjection*, pp. 8-9.
175 *Georges Bataille, Bataille On Nietzsche*, (London, 2004) p. 61.
176 *Powers of Horror: An Essay on Abjection*, p. 12.
177 Slavoj Žižek, *Interrogating the Real* (London, 2006), p. 33.
178 *American Psycho*, p. 345.
179 *American Psycho*, p. 282.
180 *Necrophilia: Forensic and Medico-legal Aspects*, p. 117.
181 *Necrophilia: Forensic and Medico-legal Aspects*, pp. 117-118.
182 *Anti-Oedipus*, p. 200.
183 Jacques Lacan, *Écrits*, (New York, 2005), p. 660.
184 *American Psycho*, p. 377.
185 The History of Sexuality, 83.
186 Dylan Evans, *An Introductory Dictionary of Lacanian Psychoanalysis* (New York, 1996), pp. 191-192.
187 *American Psycho*, p. 377.
188 *American Psycho*, p. 377.
189 *American Psycho*, p. 206.
190 *The Parallax View*, p. 182.
191 *American Psycho*, p. 377.
192 *The History of Sexuality*, p. 83.
193 *The History of Sexuality*, p. 84.
194 *The History of Sexuality*, p. 84.
195 *American Psycho*, p. 300.
196 *American Psycho*, p. 197.
197 *The History of Sexuality,* pp. 84-85.
198 *American Psycho*, p. 279.
199 *The History of Sexuality*, p. 85.
200 *American Psycho*, p. 377.

201 *The Parallax View*, p. 160.

202 *The History of Sexuality*, p. 138.

203 *American Psycho*, p. 226.

10 — NecroBanality

204 Hannah Arendt, *Eichmann in Jerusalem*, (New York, 1963)p. 253.

205 Hannah Arendt, *The Life of the Mind*, (Orlando, 1978) p. 180.

206 *A Thousand Plateaus: Capitalism and Schizophrenia*, pp. 113-114

207 *A Thousand Plateaus: Capitalism and Schizophrenia*, p. 439.

208 Fredric Jameson, 'Postmodernism, or The Cultural Logic of Late Capitalism,' *The Jameson Reader*, eds. Michael Hardt, Kathi Week (Oxford, 2000), p. 196.

209 *Crash*, p. 167.

210 *The Jameson Reader*, p. 215.

211 Denis Nilsen to Matt Ruscoff, available here: http://russcoff.typepad.com/russcoff/2004/06/cofessions_of_a.html

212 Gilles Deleuze, *AFrancis Bacon: The Logic of Sensation*, trans. Daniel W. Smith (London, 2005), p. 30.A

213 *Francis Bacon: The Logic of Sensation*, pp. 43-44.

214 Denis Nilsen to Matt Ruscoff, available here: http://russcoff.typepad.com/russcoff/2004/06/cofessions_of_a.html

215 Jeffrey Dahmer quoted in Christopher Berry-Dee, *Cannibal Serial Killers: Profiles of Depraved Flesh-Eating Murderers* (Berkeley CA, 2011), p. 149.

216 Algernon Charles Swinburne, 'Anactoria,' *Poems and Ballads & Atalanta in Calydon* (London, 2000), p. 51.

217 *Francis Bacon: The Logic of Sensation*, p. 34. Quotes within section from William S. Burroughs, *Naked Lunch*.

218 *Visions of Excess: Selected Writings, 1927-1939*, p. 132.

219 Poppy Z. Brite, *Exquisite Corpse* (New York, 1997), p. 13.

220 *Exquisite Corpse*, p.149.

11—NecroPosthuman

221 For details of Jerome Brudos's life and crimes see: Eric Hickey, *Serial Murderers and Their Victims* (Belmont, CA 1998); Ann Rule, *The Lust Killer* (New York,1988); Harold Schechter, *The Serial Killer Files* (New York, 2003); Peter Vronsky, *Serial Killers* (New York, 2004); and http://www.trutv.com/library/crime/serial_killers/predators/jerry_brudos/index.html

222 Christopher Kocela, *Fetishism and its Discontents in Post-1960 American Fiction* (New York, 2010), p. 48.

223 *Psychopathia Sexualis*, p. 22.

224 *Psychopathia Sexualis* p. 172.

225 Susana Medina, *Buñuel's Philosophical Toys* (2006)

226 Susana Medina, *Philosophical Toys* (available http://www.susanamedina.net/Susanamedina.net/Home.html)

227 *The History of Sexuality*, p. 65.

228 *Violence*, p 168.

229 *American Psycho*, p. 331.

230 Elliott Vanskike, 'Pornography as Paradox: the joint project of Hans Bellmer and Georges Bataille,' *Mosaic* (University of Manitoba, 1998).

231 'Pornography as Paradox: the joint project of Hans Bellmer and Georges Bataille.'

12—NecroCalculus

232 *Violence*, p. 48.

233 *Violence*, p. 63.

234 William T. Vollmann, *Rising Up and Rising Down*, (London, 2003), p. 1.

235 *Violence*, p. 53

236 See Ronald Milo, *Immorality*, (Princeton, 1984)

237 Terry Eagleton, *On Evil*, (New Haven, 2010), p. 107.

238 *Rising Up and Rising Down*, p. 37.

239 Chuck Palahniuk, *Lullaby* (London, 2003), p. 26.

240 Danny Kelly, *Yuck! The Nature and Moral Significance of Disgust* (London, 2011), p.28.

241 *Child Of God*, pp. 126-127.

242 *Child Of God*, p. 127.

243 Gordon Burn, *Somebody's Husband, Somebody's Son*, (London, 1984), p. 185.

244 *Somebody's Husband, Somebody's Son*, p. 305.

245 *Rising Up and Rising Down*, p. 150.

246 Slavoj Žižek, *The Pervert's Guide to Cinema*. Full transcript. http://beanhu.wordpress.com/2009/12/07/the-perverts-guide-to-cinema/

247 Winfried Menninghaus, *Disgust: The Theory and History of a Strong Sensation*, (Albany, 2003), p.1.

248 *The Psychology of Love*, p.40.

249 http://www.thesmokinggun.com/documents/crime/sex-corpse-scheme-busted

250 http://cdn.preterhuman.net/texts/anarchy_and_privacy_control/FDR/fdr-0301.txt

251 http://www.kcrg.com/news/local/51327922.html

252 http://cdn.preterhuman.net/texts/anarchy_and_privacy_control/FDR/fdr-0301.txt

253 http://cdn.preterhuman.net/texts/anarchy_and_privacy_control/FDR/fdr-0301.txt

254 *The Psychology of Love*, p.128.

255 *The Psychology of Love*, p.130.

256 *The Atrocity Exhibition*, p. 156.

257 *The Atrocity Exhibition*, p. 157.

258 Georges Bataille, quoted in *Disgust: The Theory and History of a Strong Sensation*, p. 349.

259 Rachel Herz, *That's Disgusting: Unraveling the Mysteries of Repulsion*, (New York, 2012), p. 179.

260 Friedrich Nietzsche, quoted in *Disgust: The Theory and History of a Strong Sensation*, p. 81.

261 *Violence*, p. 195.

262 Jonathan P. Rosman, MD and Phillip J. Resnick, MD, 'Sexual Attraction to Corpses: A Psychiatric Review of Necrophilia,' *Bull Am Acad Psychiatry Law, Vol. 17, No. 2,* (1989), http://www.jaapl.org/content/17/2/153.full.pdf

263 Immanuel Kant, *Groundwork for the Metaphysics of Morals,* trans. A. W. Wood, (New Haven, 2002), p. 73.

264 Friedrich Nietzsche, *On the Genealogy of Morals,* trans. Douglas Smith (Oxford, 1996), p. 65.

265 Friedrich Nietzsche, *Beyond Good and Evil,* trans. Marion Faber, (Oxford, 1998), p. 110.

266 *Rising Up and Rising Down,* p. 84.

267 *Rising Up and Rising Down,* p. 86.

268 *Rising Up and Rising Down,* p. 99.

269 *Rising Up and Rising Down,* p. 141.

270 See Aristotle, *The Nicomachean Ethics,* (Oxford, 2009).

271 Sigmund Freud, 'The Ego and the Id,' *On Metapsychology* (Middlesex, 1987), p. 380.

272 *Violence,* p. 87.

273 Irvine Welsh, *Ecstasy: Three Tales of Chemical Romance,* (London, 1996), p. 8.

13 – Necroclusion

274 Information on Nico Claux can be found here: http://web.archive.org/web/20070627053657/www.nicolasclaux.com/ and http://murderpedia.org/male.C/c/claux-nicolas.htm

275 *Erotism,* p. 92.

276 Jean-Luc Nancy, *Corpus,* trans. Richard A. Rand (New York, 2008), p. 121.

277 *The Psychology of Love,* p. 47.

278 *The Psychology of Love,* p. 101.

279 *The History of Sexuality,* p. 19.

280 Michel Foucault, *Abnormal: Lectures at the College de France 1974-1975,* trans. Graham Burchell (London, 2003), p. 94.

281 *The Psychology of Love,* p. 119.

282 *The Torture Garden*, p. 83.

283 *Corpus*, p. 77.

284 *Corpus*, p. 151.

285 *Corpus*, p. 85.

286 *The History of Sexuality*, p. 37.

287 *Disgust: The Theory and History of a Strong Sensation*, p. 194.

288 *The History of Sexuality*, p. 39.

289 *Ecstasy: Three Tales of Chemical Romance*, p. 9.

290 Stephen Barber, *England's Darkness*, (London 2013), pp. 9-10

291 *Rising Up and Rising Down*, p. 150.

292 Martin Amis, *The Information*, (London, 1995), p.28.

293 *Corpus*, p. 15.

Bibliography

Aggrawal, Anil. *Necrophilia: Forensic and Medico-Legal Aspects* (Boca Raton, 2011)

Amis, Martin. *The Information*, (London, 1995)

Arendt, Hannah. *Eichmann in Jerusalem* (New York, 1963)

Arendt, Hannah. *The Life of the Mind* (Orlando, 1978)

Aristotle, *The Nicomachean Ethics*, (Oxford, 2009)

Bachelard, Gaston. *The Poetics of Space*, trans. Maria Jolas (Boston, 1994)

Ballard, J.G. *Crash*, (London, 2008)

Ballard, J.G. *The Atrocity Exhibition* (Revised edition: London, 2006)

Barber, Stephen. *England's Darkness*, (London 2013)

Bataille, Georges. *Bataille On Nietzsche* (London, 2004)

Bataille, George. *Erotism: Death & Sensuality*, trans. Mary Dalwood (San Francisco, 1986)

Bataille, Georges. *Story of the Eye* (London, 2001)

Bataille, Georges. *Visions of Excess: Selected Writings, 1927-1939*, trans. Allan Stoekl with Carl R. Lovitt and Donald M. Leslie Jr. (Minneapolis, 1985)

Baudelaire, Charles. *Poems of Baudelaire*, trans. Roy Campbell, (New York, 1952)

Baudelaire, Charles. *Selected Poems of Charles Baudelaire*, trans. Geoffrey Wagner (New York, 1974)

Berry-Dee, Christopher. *Cannibal Serial Killers: Profiles of Depraved Flesh-Eating Murderers* (Berkeley, 2011),

Blanchot, Maurice. *The Writing of the Disaster*, trans. Ann Smock (Lincoln, 2005)

Block, Iwan. *The Sexual Life of Our Time: its Relations to Modern Civilization*, trans. M. Eden Paul (London, 1909)

Brill, A. A. 'Necrophilia—Part I.' *Journal of Criminal Psychopathology* (1941)

Brite, Poppy Z. *Exquisite Corpse* (London, 1996)

Brod, Max. *Franz Kafka: a Biography*, trans. G. Humphreys Roberts and Richard Winston (New York, 1995)

Burn, Gordon. *Happy Like Murderers* (London, 1999)

Burn, Gordon. *Somebody's Husband, Somebody's Son*, (London, 1984),

Burroughs, William S. *Naked Lunch: the Restored Text* (New York, 2010)

Burrow, Colin, ed., *Metaphysical Poetry*, (London, 2006)

Buttgereit, Jörg. *Nekromantik* (1987)

Buttgereit, Jörg. *Nekromantik 2* (1991)

Critchley, Simon. *The Book of Dead Philosophers* (London, 2008)

Deleuze, Gilles. *Difference and Repetition*, trans. Paul Patton (London, 1994)

Deleuze, Gilles. *Francis Bacon: The Logic of Sensation*, trans. Daniel W. Smith (London, 2005),

Deleuze, Gilles & Guattari, Félix. *A Thousand Plateaus: Capitalism and Schizophrenia*, trans. Brian Massumi, (Minneapolis, 1987)

Deleuze, Gilles & Guattari, Félix. *Anti-Oedipus: Capitalism and Schizophrenia*, trans. Robert Hurley, Mark Seem, and Helen R. Lane (London, 2004)

Demme, Jonathan. *The Silence of the Lambs* (1991)

Diogenes Laertius. *Lives of Eminent Philosophers*, Volume 1, trans. Robert Drew Hicks (Cambridge MA, 1972)

Eagleton, Terry *On Evil* (New Haven, 2010)

Eddowes, John. *The Two Killers of Rillington Place* (New York, 1995)

Ellis, Bret Easton. *American Psycho* (London, 2006)

Ellis, Havelock. *Studies in the Psychology of Sex, Volume V: Erotic Symbolism, The Mechanism of Detumescence, The Psychic State in Pregnancy*, (Philadelphia, 1923)

Épaulard, Dr Alexis. *Vampirisme, Nécrophilie, Nécrosadisme, Nécrophagie* (Lyon, 1901)

Evans, Dylan. *An Introductory Dictionary of Lacanian*

Psychoanalysis (New York, 1996),

Ferri, Enrico. *Criminal Sociology* (1899)

Fiennes, Sophie. *The Pervert's Guide to the Cinema* (2009)

Flavius, Josephus. *Jewish Antiquities* (London, 2006)

Fleischer Richard. *Ten Rillington Place* (1970)

Foucault, Michel. *Abnormal: Lectures at the College de France 1974-1975*, trans. Graham Burchell (London, 2003)

Foucault, Michel. *The History of Sexuality, an Introduction, Volume I.* trans. Robert Hurley (New York, 1990)

Fren, Allison de. 'The Exquisite Corpse: Disarticulations Of The Artificial Female,' unpublished doctoral dissertation University Of Southern California, 2008

Freud, Sigmund. *Civilization and Its Discontents* (London, 2004)

Freud, Sigmund. *On Metapsychology* (Middlesex, 1987)

Freud, Sigmund. *The Complete Psychological Works of Sigmund Freud,* Vol. 13, trans. James Strachey (London, 2001)

Freud, Sigmund. 'Fetishism', *The Complete Psychological Works of Sigmund Freud, Vol. 21,* trans. James Strachey (London, 2001)

Freud, Sigmund, 'The Dissection of the Psychical Personality', *New Introductory Lectures on Psychoanalysis*, trans. James Strachey (New York, 1995)

Freud, Sigmund. *The Psychology of Love*, trans. Shaun Whiteside (London, 2006)

Freud, Sigmund, *The Standard Edition of the Complete Psychological Works of Sigmund Freud, Vol. 19,* trans. James Strachey (London, 2001)

Fromm, Erich. *The Anatomy of Human Destructiveness* (New York, 1973)

Grimal, Pierre. *The Dictionary of Classical Mythology* (Oxford, 1996)

Grant, Barry Keith ed. *Planks of Reason: Essays on the Horror Film* (Metuchen, NJ, 1984)

Harman, Graham. *Prince of Networks: Bruno Latour and*

Metaphysics (Melbourne, 2009)

Harman, Graham, *Towards Speculative Realism* (Ropley, Hants, 2010)

Harrison, Ben. *Undying Love: the True Story of a Passion that Defied Death* (New York, 2001)

Heidegger, Martin, *Being and Time*, trans. John Macquarrie and Edward Robinson (New York, 1962)

Herodotus, *The History*, trans. David Greene (Chicago, 1987)

Herz, Rachel, *That's Disgusting: Unraveling the Mysteries of Repulsion*, (New York, 2012)

Hickey, Eric. *Serial Murderers and Their Victims* (Belmont, CA 1998)

Hitler, Adolf. *The Essential Hitler: Speeches and Commentary*, trans. Max Domarus (Wauconda, 2007)

Jameson, Fredric. 'Postmodernism, or The Cultural Logic of Late Capitalism,' *The Jameson Reader*, eds. Michael Hardt, Kathi Week (Oxford, 2000)

Josephus, Flavius. *Jewish Antiquities* (London, 2006)

Kafka, Franz. *Metamorphosis and Other Stories*, trans. Michael Hoffman (London, 2007)

Kant, Immanuel. *Groundwork for the Metaphysics of Morals*, trans. A. W. Wood, (New Haven, 2002), p. 73.

Kasher, Aryeh and Witztum, Eliezer. *King Herod: A Persecuted Persecutor: a Case Study in Psychohistory and Psychobiography*, trans. Karen Gold (Berlin, 2007)

Kelly, Danny. *Yuck! The Nature and Moral Significance of Disgust* (London, 2011)

Kennedy, Ludovic. *Ten Rillington Place* (London, 1961)

Keppel, Robert D. *Riverman: Ted Bundy & I Hunt for the Green River Killer* (New York, 1995)

Kocela, Christopher. *Fetishism and its Discontents in Post-1960 American Fiction* (New York, 2010)

Krafft-Ebing, Richard von. *Psychopathia Sexualis*, trans. Franklin S. Klaf (New York, 1998)

Kristeva, Julia. *Powers of Horror: An Essay on Abjection*, trans. Leon

S. Roudiez (New York, 1982)

Lacan, Jacques. *Écrits* (New York, 2005)

Lacan, Jacques. *Four Fundamental Concepts of Psycho-Analysis*, ed. Jacques-Alain Miller and trans. Alan Sheridan (New York, 1978)

Lacan, Jacques. *The Seminars of Jacques Lacan: Book VII, the Ethics of Psychoanalysis 1959-1960*, ed. Jacques-Alain Miller, trans. Dennis Porter (New York, 1997)

Lacan, Jacques. 'Desire and the Interpretation of Desire in *Hamlet*,' trans. James Hulbert, *Yale French Studies* 55-56 (1977)

Land, Nick. *Fanged Noumena: Collected Writings 1987-2007* (Falmouth, 2011)

Land, Nick. *The Thirst for Annihilation, Georges Bataille and Virulent Nihilism* (London, 1992)

Lessing, Theodor. Berg, Karl. Godwin, George. *Monsters of Weimar: The Stories of Fritz Haarmann and Peter Kurten*, trans. Mo Croasdale (London, 1993)

MacCormack, Patricia. 'Necrosexuality,' *Rhizomes* 11/12, fall 2005/spring 2006, at http://www.rhizomes.net/issue11/maccor mack/index.html

McCarthy, Cormac. *Child of God* (London, 2010)

Menninghaus, Winfried. *Disgust: The Theory and History of a Strong Sensation* (Albany, 2003)

Marinetti, F.T. *Critical Writings*, trans. Doug Thompson (New York, 2006)

Marshall, Michael. *Straw Men* (New York, 2002)

Marx, Karl and Engels, Friedrich. 'The Holy Family,' *Complete Works Vol. 4*, trans. Richard Dixon and Clement Dutts (Moscow, 1975)

Marx, Karl. *The Revolutions of 1848*, (Harmondsworth, 1973)

Medina, Susana. *Buñuel's Philosophical Toys* (2006)

Metzinger, Thomas. *The Ego Tunnel: the Science of the Mind and the Myth of the Self* (New York, 2009)

Michaud, Stephen G and Aynesworth, Hugh, *Ted Bundy:*

Conversations with a Killer (Authorlink Press, 2000)

Michaud, Stephen G and Aynesworth, Hugh, *The Only Living Witness: The True Story of Serial Sex Killer Ted Bundy* (Irving, 1999)

Milo, Ronald. *Immorality*, (Princeton, 1984)

Mirbeau, Octave. *The Torture Garden*, trans. Alvah Bessie (London, 2008),

Mori, Masahiro. *The Buddha in the Robot: a Robot Engineer's Thoughts on Science and Religion*, trans. Charles S. Terry (Tokyo, 1981)

Morrison, Grant. *Supergods* (London 2011)

Morton, Jim. 'The Unrepentant Necrophile: An Interview with Karen Greenlee,' *Apocalypse Culture: Volume 1*, ed., Adam Parfrey (Portland, 1990)

Mullen, Paul E., Pathé Michele, and Purcell Rosemary, *Stalkers and Their Victims* (Cambridge, 2000)

Nabokov, Vladimir. *Speak, Memory* (London, 2000)

Nancy, Jean-Luc. *Corpus*, trans. Richard A. Rand (New York, 2008),

Nesbø, Jo. *The Bat* (London, 2012)

Nietzsche, Friedrich. *Beyond Good and Evil*, trans. Marion Faber, (Oxford, 1998)

Nietzsche, Friedrich. *On the Genealogy of Morals*, trans. Douglas Smith (Oxford, 1996)

Parthenius. *Love Stories 2*, at http://www.theoi.com/Text/Parthenius2.html#31

Quintus of Smyrna. *The Trojan Epic: Posthomerica*, trans. Alan James (Baltimore, 2007)

Palahniuk, Chuck. *Lullaby* (London, 2003)

Phillips, John. *Sade: The Libertine Novels* (London, 2001)

Poe, Edgar Allan. *Poetry and Tales* (New York, 1984)

Quintus of Smyrna, *The Trojan Epic: Posthomerica*, trans. Alan James (Baltimore, 2007)

Ramsland, Katherine. *The Mind of a Murderer: Privileged Access to the Demons That Drive Extreme Violence* (Santa Barbara, 2011)

Rendell, Ruth. *Thirteen Steps Down* (London, 2005)

Roche, Geoffrey, 'Black Sun: Bataille on Sade,' *Janus Head*, 9(1), (2006), pp. 157-80.

Rosman, Jonathan P. and Resnick, Phillip J. 'Sexual Attraction to Corpses: A Psychiatric Review of Necrophilia,' *Bull Am Acad Psychiatry Law, Vol. 17, No. 2*, (1989), http://www.jaapl.org/content/17/2/153.full.pdf

Rule, Ann. *The Stranger Beside Me* (New York, 1989)

Rule, Ann. *The Lust Killer* (New York, 1988)

Sade, Marquis de. *The Complete Marquis de Sade*, Vol. 1., trans. Dr Paul J. Gillette (Los Angeles, 2005)

Schechter, Howard. *Deviant* (New York, 1989)

Schechter, Harold, *The Serial Killer Files* (New York, 2003)

Shakespeare, William. *Hamlet* (London, 2006)

Silverman, Kaja. *Male Subjectivity at the Margins* (London, 1992)

Simpson, Keith. *Forty Years of Murder* (London, 2008)

Steele, E. D. *Palmerston and LAiberalism, 1855-1865*A(Cambridge, 1991)

Stevens, Wallace. *The Collected Poems* (New York, 1982)

Supervert, *Necrophilia Variations* (USA, 2005)

Swicegood, Tom. *Von Cosel*, (Lincoln, 2003)

Swinburne, Algernon Charles. 'Anactoria,' *Poems and Ballads & Atalanta in Calydon* (London, 2000),

Tatar, Maria. *Lustmord: Sexual Murder in Weimar Germany* (Princeton, 1997)

Thoinot, L. *Medicolegal Aspects of Moral Offenses*, trans. Arthur W. Weysse (Philadelphia, 1923)

Vanskike, Elliott. 'Pornography as Paradox: the joint project of Hans Bellmer and Georges Bataille' *Mosaic* (University of Manitoba, 1998)

Vaughan, Thomas. *The Works of Thomas Vaughan*, ed. Arthur Edward Waite (Whitefish, 2010)

Vollmann, William T. *Rising Up and Rising Down* (London, 2003),

Vollmann, William T. *The Rainbow Stories* (New York, 1989)

Vronsky, Peter. *Serial Killers* (New York, 2004)

Wallace, David Foster, *Both Flesh and Not* (London, 2012)

Watson, Peter. *The German Genius* (London, 2010)

Weismantel, Mary. 'Moche Sex Pots: Reproduction and Temporality in Ancient South America,' *American Anthropologist*, Vol. 6, No. 3, (September 2004)

Welsh, Irvine. *Ecstasy: Three Tales of Chemical Romance*, (London, 1996),

Wilson, Colin. *A Criminal History of Mankind* (London, 2005)

Winnicott, Donald. 'Transitional Objects and Transitional Phenomena – a Study of the First Not-me Possession,' *International Journal of Psycho-Analysis*, 34 (1953)

Woods, Paul Anthony. *Ed Gein – Psycho!* (New York, 1995)

Wulffen, Erich, *Enzyklopadie de Modernen Kriminalistik* (Berlin, 1910)

Žižek, Slavoj. *How to Read Lacan,* (London, 2006)

Žižek, Slavoj. *Interrogating the Real* (London, 2006),

Žižek, Slavoj. *The Parallax View* (Cambridge, 2009)

Žižek, Slavoj. *Violence* (New York, 2008)

Contemporary culture has eliminated both the concept of the public and the figure of the intellectual. Former public spaces – both physical and cultural – are now either derelict or colonized by advertising. A cretinous anti-intellectualism presides, cheerled by expensively educated hacks in the pay of multinational corporations who reassure their bored readers that there is no need to rouse themselves from their interpassive stupor. The informal censorship internalized and propagated by the cultural workers of late capitalism generates a banal conformity that the propaganda chiefs of Stalinism could only ever have dreamt of imposing. Zer0 Books knows that another kind of discourse – intellectual without being academic, popular without being populist – is not only possible: it is already flourishing, in the regions beyond the striplit malls of so-called mass media and the neurotically bureaucratic halls of the academy. Zer0 is committed to the idea of publishing as a making public of the intellectual. It is convinced that in the unthinking, blandly consensual culture in which we live, critical and engaged theoretical reflection is more important than ever before.